LA BELLE FRANCE • BESSIE RAYNER BELLOC

ᜊ ᜊ ᜊ ᜊ ᜊ ᜊ ᜊ ᜊ

LA BELLE FRANCE -
By BESSIE PARKES-BELLOC
AUTHOR OF "VIGNETTES," ETC.
w'r *avoir. Allons courir!*
Vie errante
Est chose enivrante.
Voir c'est avoir. Allons courir t
Car tout l'Oit c'est tout conquérir.
DE KftKANQKK
LONDON
DALDY, ISBISTER & CO.
56, LUDGATE HILL
187;
Harvard College Library, Nov. 14, i801. LOWELL BBQUH8T.
MADAME LOUISE SWANTON-BELLOC BY HER SON'S WIFE. CONTENTS.

INTRODUCTION.

Composed from an antiquarian and poetical point of view only, these pic-tures of the provincial towns of France aim at nothing but the preserving for English readers some traces of that wonderful beauty which is yearly van-ishing like a dream; and which, inas-much as it was the result of a vigorous independence, fecund in every depart-ment of national life, merits a far more elaborate and artistic treatment. But, at least, my papers should possess a cer-tain freshness; as they were all written either on the localities of which they speak, or immediately after I had quit-ted them, and while the impressions I had received were fresh in my mind.

Twenty years ago the strong *cachet* of the Middle Ages yet remained in the French provinces. '93 had torn up the ancient civilization hy the roots, hut, like a forest tree felled in full leaf, the branches yet continued green, and their ruins still cumbered the mossy soil, so that one might perceive where the state-ly growth had been. The Eevolution of July always appears to me to have been more destructive, because it was pur-sued to its results with far more cal-culation. For instance, it was in 1832 that the monumental beauty of Sens was destroyed; and the municipalities under Louis Philippe pulled down and rebuilt, and swept and garnished, in obedience to ideas which told more heavily on what remained of ancient France, than did the mad violence of the Great Eevo-lution. 1830 took up the broken thread of 1789, and pieced it with its own new skein; until, in 1848, the whole snapped, as ever, at the weakest part. But the great destructor, from which there is at once no appeal, and, after which, no possibility of restoration, is the spirit of the present age embodied in the actual ruling power. When I walk through the enormous streets and boulevards of New Paris, I feel appalled by the change, and even unable to dispute with it mentally; for it bears the imprint of an idea which is becoming dominant over Europe, and which, little as I love it, I feel forced to accept with as much good grace as may be; for it is evidently the *condition* of the future. For the moment, the individuality of man, as expressed in his dwelling and physical arrangements, is gone,—suppressed. The human creature no longer builds for himself, decorates for himself; no longer lets loose his fancy, his humour, his notions of the fitting and comfortable. Science and economy—at least economy as regards the facile production of a certain degree of luxury—go hand in hand, and lay down his streets and erect his houses.

I cannot deny that the average citizen gains thereby in many important respects; and as, after all, the essential germ of each soul differs from every other soul as much now as in the days when Jacques Coeur expended the wealth of his imagination upon his dwelling-house, till it rose to tell the whole story of the inner and the outer man, —we must hope that the living vigour of humanity will break through the excessive monotony of modern arrangements, and assert itself in new forms, which may cause the new generation to feel less regret at heing compelled to Avalk in a straight line three miles long, from the Luxembourg to the Chemin-de-Fer du Nord.

None the less precious, however, is every trace of the old order. It grew in so rich a soil of faith, it expanded in such various directions, it founded as we cannot found, it created such tough, vital groups of men and women. The towns of the Middle Ages, having so much less advantage of participation than their modern descendants, were forced to provide their own speeches, their own acts, and, to a certain extent, their own heroes. Assisi is redolent of St. Francis, Sienna of St. Catherine, Dinan of Duguesclin, Orleans of Jeanne d'Arc. But owing to the immense scope of the means of intercourse and communication, our modem great men are

for all space, long before we can decide whether or not they will be for all time! One of the very few names we can associate in modern days as being indissolubly bound up with a place, is that of the Curd d'Ars, and to Ars pious Catholics go in pilgrimage, holding the place holy for the sake of the man. It is partly this curious loosening of the sense of locality which makes very sensible people, when they are not moved by any religious feeling in the matter, seriously consider that the Pope could govern the Catholic Church with as much facility away from Eome,—anywhere, in fact, where the post or the telegraph could bring the ecclesiastical news of the world to his feet. They think that the Catholic Church should loosen her hold upon the material world, and should neither build nor endow.

The same spirit makes no account of the parochial organization of the English Church, but would trust everything to the ideas communicated to the people by the education of books, which are of all things the most curiously devoid of *body,* when we consider the amount of thought which can be bound up in one volume, and that it can be—not copied or imitated— but identically reproduced any number of times, in any number of places.

But this tendency to reduce all life to interchangeable forms, which is often loudly praised, and not unrightly, for bringing the result of one intelligence within the reach of all, is incessantly combated by an instinct of the human heart which venerates the relic, the shrine, the outward expression; and the two principles can he seen struggling together very curiously in America. Of all interchangeable places American towns must be the most so. A "city" grows up West with the celerity of a conjuror's trick. Ready-made houses, ready-made streets, ready-made citizens and institutions. Not for them are the slow, heroic struggles of Bruges, or Ghent, or the rings which mark the changes of the bark in the royal oak of an English town.

Yet it is from America that Washington Irving comes to paint 'Bracebridge

Hall;' from America that Longfellow brings that marvellously delicate appreciation of old Germany, which makes the reading of 'Hyperion ' the fit companion for floating in a fairy vessel down the Rhine. America gave us Hawthorne, who hungered and thirsted for the ancient and the romantic, and who has linked the past and the present together in the 'House of the Seven Gables,' with a sort of ghostly skill. Who ever meets an American who is willing to leave the old land without going to Stratford-on-Avon? The refined and imaginative class in the United States long for that which they have not got—the spreading roots of the past. Protestants as they are in the grain, they flock to Eome with delight, they flock to the ceremonies, they spend great sums on photographs, bronzes, and costly books. They are a people of elegant antiquarians—I speak of the rich and of the cultivated people, of Boston especially.

The same spirit prevails in a section of English society. About the same time that the municipality of Sens were pulling down churches and gates and walls, Lord Herbert of Lea was forming the first tastes which led him to build his church at Wilton, and adorn it with every rarity of ecclesiastical art; and the Oxford School were laying the foundation of the High Church movement, and of the great Catholic revival of the last twenty years; both of which tend to the localizing of life. While one sort of man travels every other day from Manchester to London, another sort of man becomes a Passionist monk, and a third builds up a lovely church in a green hollow of the Hampshire downs.

It is with humanity as with nature: the mobile forces which geologists tell us are constantly at work, changing the external world, are mixed with the forces which preserve the same types in constant reproduction through long ages. Nevertheless, the last century has been for man an era of change, which it is difficult to believe has a parallel in his past history. It is science which is changing the face of outward things, and enabling vast operations to be undertaken with such amazing celerity. But things which can be done quickly can also be undone quickly; and the great new boulevards, and the monster hotels, even though they be built of solid marble or neatest brick, entirely lack that air of solidity which is possessed by the arch of a thirteenth-century chapel, or by the low sturdy stone cottage of the peasant among the Yorkshire hills.

That which is really durable in our great modern erections is the idea, the mathematical principle upon which they repose, and which is so completely master of the situation that it can transform the outward result at its will. We stand with amazement before the Pont du Gard, or before the gigantic wall of the Theatre at Orange; enormous in their own proportions, they typify the power of the Roman nation which raised them for the convenience of its colonial subjects; and they have lasted fifteen hundred years. The huge railway viaduct of Morlaix is bigger; it is the most gigantic erection I ever saw or conceived of; it spans the valley and the river and a part of the town with a monstrous stride: but it does not impress me, and I doubt if it will ever impress any one, with the same sense of vastness and durability as the Pont du Gard. We know that it was built by modern engineers for the railway to pass in one particular line. If twenty years hence some new invention made it desirable for the railway to pass three miles up or two miles down the river, that huge viaduct would be taken to pieces like a bridge of child's bricks, and moved to the new place!

A sense of repose and stability is therefore to be found in the older things, which to some states of mind constitutes their greatest charm. The imagination, which by their aid can travel back into the past, is thereby delivered temporarily from the anxieties and agitations of the present. Deep must be the grief, or profound the mental disquiet, which cannot be soothed by plunging into a completely different set of associations. It is as much as to say that the effort cannot be made. For me there is no uneasiness which would not be at least calmed by such a recurrence to the life of former ages. This is, of course, a mental habit, capable of being cherished or discouraged. A man may dwell in the actual till all calmness disappears from his face, his gestures, and his speech, and he betrays by his restlessness that present interests are all in all; or he may absorb himself in the past until he becomes a dreaming antiquarian; or in the abstract and the unseen until he attains the higher forms of metaphysic or mathematic thought; or, in religion, of the contemplative life. But there is *un juste milieu* in ordinary nature, and it is certain that a taste for historic study is a great help to mental cheerfulness, and to seeing things in their due proportion.

One of the many reasons why a great gothic church soothes those who go to pray there, is the feeling that it is a universal home; that the worshippers of today are but the descendants and inheritors of those who moved across its pavement in past centuries,—the parents of those who will visit its altars in days to come. Shall we dare to fling ourselves in impatient agony against those mighty walls,—upon that patient floor? Hearts which do not put this feeling clearly to themselves, are yet stilled by its influence, subdued by its chastening power. The mind and the soul are curiously allied, they are affected by correspondent influences. "Peace is the proper result of the Christian temper; it is the great kindness which our religion doth us, that it brings us to a settledness of mind and a consistency within ourselves," and a part of this *peace* springs not only from a habit of submission to the divine will, but from a habit of thinking of the individual life as part of the great whole of the Church, whereby the temporal sorrows and struggles are dwarfed in the imagination. Could the historian of the 'Monks of the West' have absorbed himself in personal ambition while writing that book, or while he was wandering over France in search of the ruined foundations of its monasteries? Not far from Aries is a hill covered with the ruins of ecclesiastical buildings; it is the *Mont Majeur* of the Benedictines, and from its walls can be seen a wonder *b* ful view of the flat valley of the Rhone, the towers of Aries in the mid distance. I saw Mont Majeur on a soft grey day in early spring; the level landscape lay in tender hues of grey and purple, aud its scene of vastness and of peace went to my heart. It was a fitting frame for those studious lives. The railway passes now between that hill and Aries. I would that Mont Majeur were claimed by its old inhabitants, and that the passengers in that express train, by which so many of us have so often travelled, might see from its windows, not the protest but the counterbalance to their busy errands, and their world-embracing voyages from the populous port below.

The exceeding beauty of the old French architecture is another reason for wandering through these provincial towns at leisure. It is not only that the ecclesiastical gothic of the age of St. Louis is so marvellous for its lightness and grandeur. We can rival it at home; to me Canterbury and Westminster remain unsurpassed, and the village churches of England have a quiet grace and beauty which is all their own. But the French domestic buildings of every class, from the fortified castle to the humblest house deemed worthy of stone, seem to have had a poet for their architect; and in many of the towns the old cathedrals and large churches are losing much of their charm, owing to the perverse passion for clearing great spaces round them, instead of leaving them to rise up as of old from among the pointed roofs and turrets of the habitations at their feet. Nantes has suffered in this way to a deplorable extent; the vast west front looks down on a square desolation, and heaven knows what is going to be rebuilt or planted; perhaps a garden with gilt railings; perhaps a monster hotel; and at the moment at which I write, Notre Dame de Paris sits almost alone upon its island, looking in the distance like some huge couchant animal, all the inexpressible beauty of its position sacrificed. If one could believe that the streets on the island would be rebuilt with some reference to the mighty lines of Notre Dame, one might not regret the inevitable changes which take place in a great city, which is constantly developing fresh wants; but the masses of new erections on the neighbouring quays give us small hope of that. Seen from the Pont Royal, their flat bare outlines have done their best to spoil the most beautiful architectural picture in the world.

But let us be thankful for what remains. Far and wide, over Burgundy, Brittany, and Touraine;—in the sea-side towns of Normandy and Picardy, and in the sunburnt plains of Provence, are still to be found the beautiful traces of the genius of the Middle Ages. I recall the nooks and corners of the city of Sens, where the pigeons sit on the grey wall-tops, sunning themselves among the golden gilly flowers, with St. Etienne in the background, taking ever some new expression with every changing cloud;—I remember the overarching stories of the streets of Vannes and Quimper, where the rich stone of the renaissance shows like a sumptuous intrusion on the quaint modern gables of an earlier age, which still surround it on every side. I remember Guingamp, where revolution and improvement have vainly conspired to destroy all the picturesqucness of its ancient sites, and quaint Morlaix, with its old houses incrustcd with saints and angels. I remember Tarascon and Avignon, each with a touch of Italy in their massive lines, and Dijon and Tours, both full of the stately and suitable buildings of the age of Louis XIV., intermingled with the earlier style; charming Mantes, where the Seine flows underneath that fair white church of St. Louis, and where Henri Quatre made his head-quarters; Abbeville and Dieppe, less changed than many a town in the far interior, full of quaint houses, each with its great grey House of Prayer. All these I have seen, with sketch-book in hand, and, if possible, a local guide-book, compiled by some enthusiastic son of the soil, who utters reflections of withering scorn upon his municipality and their improvements, and digs with a reverent painstaking hand into the archives of his native place. There are few towns in France about which somebody has not

written an enthusiastic book, and one which it is necessary to buy if one would understand the scene. The local works on Sens, Eheims, Guingamp, and Abbeville recur to my mind as especially delightful. That of Eheims is illustrated by a small panoramic map of the ancient city three hundred years ago; it is full of the most curious local details of the Eevolution, some of which I have extracted. That of Abbeville is nearly, if not quite, out of print; it is in two volumes: I found it in the Town Museum, and again in the Imperial Library of Paris. That of Sens is compiled with careful details of the Eoman occupation, and with small engravings of some of the Roman antiquities which I should have been glad to have been able to reproduce. As to the history of Guingamp, it is written with a passion of affection which is extremely touching. The little town lives in its pages through all its centuries of vivacious existence; and its registers and public accounts have been raked for illustrative details. There isjiot hardly a square league in all this wide land whose story would not be full of a similar interest, could we but investigate it in a similar spirit; for this nation has had a vigorous life in every member. The late independence of the French provinces preserved their local parliaments— their local courts of all kind. For four hundred years after the conquest of England by the Normans, Brittany preserved her freedom; and long after the marriage of its princess to the king of France, its people struggled for their own laws and customs. Mme. de Sevignd, whose sympathies were all on the side of France, gives a lively picture of the Due de Chaulnes' difficulties as governor; and of Mme. de Chaulnes' exceeding disgust at her long exile from Paris in consequence thereof. Of the rising in 1720 I have attempted a slight sketch in the one little talc which this book contains; the story of the "Brothers Talhouet" is a simple matter of local history, and the heart-broken letter of the widow of the youngest is but the literal translation of the one she actually wrote to her confessor—it bearing in every line the impress of ter-

rible truth. In fact, Brittany never bent to the metropolis of the kingdom. "When Paris was loyal to subserviency, the province poured out her good blood in assertion of her ancient privileges, When Paris slew its good and gentle king, Brittany rose, en masse, for the rights of his successor. Only last year I was talking to a Breton nobleman, a Legitimist pur sang, whose father had been a staunch adherent of the Duchesse de Berri; I asked him what he would wish for Brittany had he the power of disposing of public events; I expected he would reply, that he desired simply the return of the elder Bourbon to the throne of France: instead of which, said he, "I desire the return of the King, and Brittany restored to all her ancient and independent laws and privileges, as in the days of the Duchess Anne!" Here, it must be confessed, Was constancy to a political idea!

Owing to its geographical position, the western province retained its individuality longer than any other; it was also somewhat longer its own mistress, having heen annexed by marriage in 1491; but Burgundy was a semi-independent duchy only twelve years previously, having been annexed by Louis Onzc, who likewise possessed himself of Provence, hitherto held by the successors of Charles of Anjou, King of Naples, and which still retains the traces of Italy in its architecture, and its marked patois.

To all English travellers who seek somewhat more in France than the gay bustle of the Rue do Eivoli, the limits of her ancient provinces arc the essential outlines of the map; each has its separate story and each its separate charm. And to the good favour of all such kind travellers I commend my book, as indicating the sources of interest which surround their every footstep, as soon as the Channel waves have landed them upon that grey line of cliff and shore, which, to one who stands by Dover Castle, shines so brightly in the setting sun!

La Ckllk St. Cloud,
February 20, 1868.
AN OLD FRENCH CITY.

Y a special interposition of Providence, and the prayers *(aous entendu)* of its patron saint, St. Etienne, Bourges is on the road to nowhere. It is approached, in this year of grace eighteen hundred and sixty-seven, by a little branch railway between the *Litjne da Centre* and the *Ligne du Boarbonnais*. It is also built upon a small hill, overlooking the wide plains of

H6tel Lallemand.

Berri; in consequence it would be both expensive and useless to drive boulevurts through its antique streets. It therefore remains much what it was twenty years ago, when we drove into the town with posthorses, being bound from Geneva to Paris. Oh! those days of trotting horses and jingling bells, across the bare wide fields of France; along the interminable *paces* lined with low fruit-trees; past the dirty villages, each with its small hostelerie, and its little church; and so at night clattering into the gates of the fortified town! Those days are gone for ever. I am glad I have known them. "I, too, have been in Arcadia," and have driven post like Sterne, like Arthur Young, like Louis XVI. flying to Varennes, like Marie Antoinette looking in agonized suspicion from her chariot window. You, my little heir of the nineteenth century! you, 0 child of the train and the telegraph! nothing will you ever know of ancient France — of *l'ancien regime.* You will not even stop at towns such as these; for you will have no youthful memories calling on you to "*halte-la!*" To you, Bourges, Chartres, Rheims, will simply mean *"Buffet, ili. c minutes d'arret."* 0 child of the nineteenth century, 1 pity you from the depths of my heart!

Now, for the moment, we have to do with Bourges—how to get there? It cost me some trouble to find out, so excuse me if I explain. You go to Orleans—that is simple enough; Orleans is on the high-road to everywhere; meaning the Loire, Tours, Nantes; or the Spanish frontier, by Poitiers, Angouleme, and Bordeaux. But to come here you go to none of these places. You get out at Orleans, and into a slow little train, which creeps over an interminable marshy heath, reminding one of Chat Moss, that

triumph of English engineers. Presently you come to Vierzon, and here again you diverge on to another and still less important line, which in an hour's time deposits you at Bourges.

"Bourges, then," observes the untravelled, "is an unimportant place after all. What do you go there for *V Pardon;* Bourges is the ancient capital of Berri; and you know, or ought to know, that the father of the legitimate king of France derived his title hence. The father of the exiled Henry V., commonly called Comte de Chambord, was Due de Berri. He was assassinated in 1821, and his widow was that heroic Madame of whom such exciting stories are yet told in Brittany. She only died in 1864, a brave woman, who would have saved France, so far as she knew, from endless troubles and a doubtful future—*tovjours h recommencer.*

Secondly, Berri is the native country of perhaps the second greatest French author of this century. I give the first place to Honore de Balzac, the second to Georges Sand. She loves it, and has given the most charming descriptions of its familiar landscape. She has an estate therein, where she lives like a Lady Bountiful; one of the many phases of her many-sided nature.

Thirdly, Bourges possesses one of the four great cathedrals of France; Amiens, Kheims, Chartres, are the other three.

Fourthly, Bourges has a particular association for the British public. They do not know much of French history, it is true; the grand, the picturesque, the romantic scroll, which descends from Pepin and Charlemagne to the feet of the last lone and childless son of the Fleur de Lys, is almost an unknown writing to the Englishman, who yet can boast of Alfred, of the Black Prince, and great Queen Bess; but there is *one* French king, immortalized by Sir Walter Scott in his ' Quentin Durwardand familiarized by Charles Kean, at the Princess's Theatre; with whom we are all acquainted. His crafty intellect, his superstitious devotion, his peculiar cap with the metal images of saints, his abominable hypocrisy, his love of the Scotch Mercenaries, and the clever way

in which he began to assert the predominance of the monarchical power above that of the feudal *scujneurs,*—all these things are pretty well known to the reading and the playgoing public. Well, Louis XI. was born at Bourges; his father, Charles VII., the king whose kingdom was saved by Jeanne d'Arc, was driven here by the English, and so beset that at one time he was more rightly to be called king of Bourges only, than king of that France which was really in the hands of his natural enemies, our honourable selves. Such are the titles of Bourges to a respectful interest. They would look well in a gazetteer; they occupy a couple of pages in Murray's 'Handbook of France;' but what geography, what handbook, can ever give the least idea of the living beauty and interest of these old French cities? To define their charms is as difficult as to say why peaches ripen. It is not only beauty, though they are rich in that; I saw to-day the cathedral of Bo urges rise flat and grey across a patch of water bordered by tall poplars, and marvelled at its adaptation to all accessories; to a foreground of gardens, and equally to its architectural approaches by gable-ended streets. But it is not beauty only. It is tradition, romance, the regretful sense of that which is fast disappearing. It is reverence for our fathers, anxiety for generations to come; it is the idea and the charm of the past, the present, and the undeveloped future, all wrapt in one vision of other days.

First and foremost, of the Cathedral of Bourges. How shall one translate it into words? A few zigzags from the inspired pencil of Pugin would better suffice. Yes, even better than a photograph, for Pugin gave in his sketches not merely the beauty of the thing represented, but his own vivid appreciation of it; so that in looking at his marvellous sketches of foreign architecture one seems to see it with Pugin's eyes.

All day, from morning to evening, I have been in and out of this cathedral, examining its details by the help of a very good guide, written by one of its own clergy—written, consequently, as a man writes of his native land. Well, then, the present edifice is the fourth of its name and race, the first having been built A.d. 250, in the days of Roman GaulThe legend says that St. Ursiu, the apostle of Berri, and first archbishop of Bourges, was allowed to build it on the ground of the Roman Palace, or Governor's House. It was rebuilt in a.D. 380 by another saint, and again in the ninth century. Some fragments of this last erection yet remain, but the glorious church now called St. Etienne de Bourges was built early in the thirteenth century, in what we call the "Early English" style. Perhaps it is our familiarity with its long sombre lines which makes it so inexpressibly beautiful to English eyes.

The construction is singular, the external situation eminently picturesque; high above the ramparts at the extreme south-east of the town, and having a large garden crossed by avenues of limes between it and the wall. It is a long building, without transepts, and with a double aisle on each side of the nave; the mid walk thus formed having been intended for processions. The perspective flies away like that of Westminster Abbey, and is lost in a glimmer of painted glass. The pillars arc immensely high, and their plain simplicity increases the effect; some architects have even objected to the extraordinary height; but their defence is that they "lift up the hearts" of the beholder. *Sursum eorda* is their everlasting response.

Then the number of these columns—they form a forest of stone. Taking them altogether, large and little, and counting those composite ones of which Sir Walter Scott says that at Melrose they were—

"Like bundles of lances which garlands had bound," there are nearly three thousand, and almost every capital is carefully and beautifully designed and sculptured. Therefore the effect, when one walks across the west end, from wall to wall, may be.imagined. "The groves," says Bryant—

"The groves were God's first temples. Ere man learned
To hew the shaft, or lay the architrave,
And spread the roof above them; ere he framed
The lofty vault to gather and roll back
The sound of anthems,—in the darkling wood,
Amidst the cool and silence, he knelt down,
And offered to the Mightiest solemn thanks
And supplication."

But here is a temple which wellnigh realizes the effect of those primitive groves, and it is perhaps due to its imposing height and the vast scale and simple breadth even of its detail, that it is much less *molested* by false ornament of a temporary kind than most foreign cathedrals. Here are no bad pictures, no gilded constructions of the taste of Louis lo Grand. All belongs to the earlier and purer epochs of French art. The altars are small, and such of them as are modern have been restored after ancient models. The images of saints in the chapels which surround the exterior aisle are small, and of a refined character; and the wroughtiron work which separates the choir from the nave is extremely delicate. Thus there is nothing to distract the eye from the great architectural conceptions here so wonderfully carried out. And through this vast building the population ebbs and flows all the Sunday like the waves of the sea. I spent nearly the whole day in the cathedral, examining the chapels between the services, and was much struck by the way in which it was really used by the people. Cold as was the weather, it had a warm look. In the afternoon the mighty nave was paved with a dense mass of human beings, to hear a preacher from Paris. The men had the advantage, being grouped in the neighbourhood of the pulpit. Outside them, on every side, were the white caps of the Bcrrichon women, intermingled with the bonnets of the fashionable ladies. About five o'clock the great congregation broke up, streaming through the several doors to the thunder of the organ, as twilight began to darken the aisles, which are always dim, even at noon, so rich is the painted glass. It was spared in "'93," because it would have been so expensive to reglaze even with white glass. But eighteen windows were sacrificed, I believe, in the middle of the last century, because the worshippers could not see to read their prayer-books—a remote consequence of the invention of printing! The painted windows which remain arc covered with Bible stories. They are among the most beautiful in the world.

There is a subterranean church, which hardly deserves to be called a crypt, so fair and lightsome is it. It contains some monuments, finely sculptured, which were deposed from the upper church in "'93." I need not say that from the tower one sees far and wide over Bourges and the flat plains of Berri, where the vine is largely cultivated.

Then I went over the roofs of each aisle, there being a considerable space (as in the dome of St. Paul's) between that which is seen from below and the exterior. Oh, the enormous masonry! oh, the forest of beams! All strong, and straight, and smooth, and six hundred years old. A real forest must have been sacrificed to build St. Etienne. This walk was agreeably diversified by crawling up a stone staircase, with wide iron rails, outside one of the flying buttresses. It was not till we had moved considerably to one side that I had any conception where we had been,—passing through the mid-air on a narrow, sloping bridge of stone, which looked a mere nothing. "Everybody asks to go up that staircase," said the good Suisse triumphantly. Query, whether they wish to do so *twice*. I am glad to say we came down from the roof quite another way, or I think I should have stayed up there unto this hour.

On the Monday morning I threaded the narrow winding streets, in which a stranger inevitably loses his way, until I found the second antiquarian treasure of this old city,—the magnificent mansion of Jacques Coeur, the Gresham of France. It is such a famous place, this "house that Jacques built," that every child in Bourges will point you the way.

If I were a rich merchant, with galleys upon every sea and trucks upon every railroad (since one should suit one's illustrations to the times in which one lives), I can imagine nothing more delightful than the building for myself a palace such as this commercial prince of the middle ages built for himself and his people; a home which, from top to toe, from balustraded roof to deep cellar, was symbolical of his name, his trade, his tastes, his very humours. His dwelling must have fitted Jacques Cocur as its skin fits an animal. All its quaint architectural corners seem, as it were, wrinkles and creases, whereby it adapted itself to the nature and genius of the man. We, in our day, know nothing of such a style of building. If we want a large house we send for an architect, who submits his plans to our enlightened judgment; allotting ample stairs, a sufficiency of best bedrooms, kitchen, butler's pantry, etc. If rather less, then rather cheaper; and as to making the slightest difference in style on account of our late pursuits, as whether, for instance, we were a retired candlestick-maker, or a lord chancellor, or a physician,—the very idea would savour of lunacy. *Sgalite, fraternity,*—are we not all alike in our stature, in our physical wants, in our deep content with bricks and mortar? Let us build and plaster our houses into uniformity with our own tails, like the beavers, only with somewhat less *finesse* and ingenuity. We know already what the result will be; we run no unknown risk. It will be Baker Street on a small scale, Victoria Street on a large one.

Not so Jacques Coeur. This man wished, in dying, to leave a beautiful shell behind him, so that the passers-by might say, " Here lived a great merchant; he had a wife, sons, and a daughter, and numerous domestics. He liked his money, but loved art more; he kept a negro; he was pious, also loyal. He didn't mind fighting, if needs must be; but preferred commerce and politics. He loved Bourges, and Bourges loved him; for he paid his workmen well." All this, and more, Jacques Coeur contrived to write in legible characters on the walls of his house, some of it on the outside, some of it on the inside. To this day it testifies what manner of man he was,—own brother to Whittington and to Gre-

sham; akin to the princes of Venice and of Holland; a man of manifold energies, who abided by his family motto, "*a vaillants Cceurs riens impossible.*"

The pedestrian traveller, while pursuing the narrow street which bears his wholly plebeian name (James Heart, neither more nor less), turns suddenly through the ornamental gateway, whose door is adorned with an elaborate knocker, the hammer of which strikes upon a *heart;* and stands transfixed in that elaborate court, asking, " But who was he, this man of ample wealth and ampler brain?" It is easy to answer. He was a contemporary of Jeanne d'Arc, and did for his king, by his gold, what she did by faith and the sword. Jacques Coeur and the Maid of Orleans may be represented as upholding the crown of France in those days. Charles VII. was not worth either of their devotions, and Providence probably considered his abominable ingratitude in bestowing upon him Louis XI. for a son. Jacques Coeur was born at Bourges, his father being largely engaged in trade. Jacques wedded, while quite a young man, the daughter of the provost; her name was Macee de Leopart. When he built his house he paid due honour to his wife, whose portrait and family arms appear in several places. He extended his father's trade immensely; was concerned in the coinage both of Bourges and Paris—a sort of master of the mint; and his thoughts were engrossed by large schemes of commerce, full of their own poetry; for in 1152 he went to the East, to make personal acquaintance with men and places, and on his return to France he fixed his commercial headquarters at Montpellier, covered the Mediterranean with his ships, and had agents and commercial travellers in all directions, many of whom afterwards became eminent, testifying to the sagacity of his choice. Does this little description convey the idea of a real man? Not a mere historical figure, buried in dry words; but a genuine creature, rising from honour to honour; lending only too much money to his king, sent on delicate foreign missions, even to the Pope; getting so alarmingly rich that

jealous people naturally desired his fall and pickings.

In person he was slightly and nervously framed; his face was very peculiar, and he had an astonishing forehead. Except that there was a strong development of the imaginative element about the temples, this countenance suggests to the modern beholder somewhat of a likeness to Lord Brougham. It docs not add to the *unity* of his portrait that he caused himself to be drawn in the guise of an angel, with tall wings and a quantity of yellow hair flying behind. That was *une petite fantaisie du moyen dge;* the unmistakable visage is there all the same.

This ugly genius being, as aforesaid, enormously rich, bought, in the year 1445, about four hundred and twenty-two years ago, a piece of land situated on the ramparts of the town, and set to work to build. Tradition says his house cost him a hundred thousand golden crowns, which is, I believe, somewhere about £240,000. On the *outside,* that which backed upon the rampart and moat, it took the shape and aspect of a fortress; on the town side it literally broke out into blossom. The accompanying woodcut is necessarily on too small a scale to give other than an idea of the general effect of the court. It is *covered* with symbolic sculpture, or with domestic portraiture. For instance, the panels of the pointed tower upon the left are each occupied by two servants, women sweeping with brooms (new, let us hope); small retainers; a female, the housekeeper perhaps, giving alms to a beggar; and halfway np are himself and his wife. He holds a hammer, the symbol of industry, called by a French proverb *la clef des arts.* Over the kitchen door (right in the corner, with little steps leading up to it) is a sculptured panel of cooks and scullions, busy over their fire. One would need long ladders and good eyes to enter into the spirit of these strange bas-reliefs, which are of the funniest, the most familiar description. Of course his handsomest room looked into this court, and in the recess over the entrance he set up a figure of himself, riding upon his mule.

The chapel is within this gateway; it was very high before it was barbarously divided into two storeys. You see the window shooting up to the roof. Here it was that Jacques caused Italian artists to paint himself, his wife, his children, and various relations, all in the guise of adoring angels.

It is not to be supposed that Jacques Coeur could spend much time in his handsome receptiou-rooms. When at home, he appropriated to himself certain little round rooms in that strong tower at the back. The view is taken from what *was* the moat, now the Place de Berri. Observe that there are no windows near the bottom. Some way up is his study, his little domestic office, where he wrote his letters and did up his accounts. Above that, fenced from the staircase by a strong iron door and wonderful lock, which still works unwearied after four hundred years of duty, was his vaulted strong-room. It is said he had a hole made in the floor, through which he could pitch his money and himself down into his study, supposing that robbers were attacking his strong-room. The corbels in this room are extraordinary. One is said to reveal the secrets of his future disgrace,—an interview, political perhaps, with Agnes Sorel, the king's mistress, to which the king was a concealed party, perched up in a tree. Jacques is represented as becoming suddenly aware of the king's presence by seeing his face reflected in a fountain. It is impossible to say if this is the true interpretation of this quaint bit of sculp ture. There is something peculiarly whimsical in the-idea of Jacques causing it to be portrayed in his secret strong-room, as if to remind him of possible dangers in the future.

Above this room runs an external gallery, of which the balustrade is ornamented with alternate hearts and cockleshells, indicative of pilgrimage. Here he came into near neighbourhood of the chimneys, and consequently he trimmed their tops with the most delicate stone frills. And along the roof line he laid a neat cover or hem of lead, which he gilded with hearts and cockle-shells, and here and there a little statue, such

as that of monk, knight, or pilgrim. Under the eaves of the observatory chamber is a portrait of his negro, hugging his coffer; and a little further on, an angel affably holding his coat of arms. A shield near at hand bears the arms of another rich commercial family allied to his own,—fleurs-de-lys interspersed with bales of silk or wool. In a similar spirit, the roof of a fine gallery is neither more nor less in construction than the reversed keel of a ship; and the massive chimney-piece represents a fortress, and has two little dormer windows atop, with folks looking out of them.

Now, does not the home represent the man? Is it not full of him even to the present hour? Fancy him showing all these queer or poetical devices to his admiring friends! Fancy Madame Coeur and her maidens going busy about the household work amidst their own portraits, and their own coats of arms, and their own mottoes, smiling at them from every door-post and window-sill! Jacques Coeur was great in the way of mottoes. Besides his chief one, which he sculptured on a balcony overlooking the street—

"A vaillants Coeurs riens impossible," he had two others, deeply characteristic of the man he must have been. This—

"A close bouclie,
II n'entre mouehe;"
and this—

"Entendre, taire,
Dire, et faire,
Est ma joie."

And now for a sad ending to so great a man; sad in that he was uprooted from his native place, and died an exile, though he found a glorious death. He fell into disgrace with his king,—probably because he had lent him too much money. He was arrested, and his property fell temporarily into the hands of the monarch, but was afterwards partially disgorged, and one of his sons got possession of this splendid dwelling. He himself, accused of several crimes, such as coining bad money, selling arms to the infidels (that was how they treated a matter of steam-rams in those days), pressing men to man his ships, selling

a Christian slave who had taken refuge with one of his captains, etc. etc., was condemned to banishment and confiscation. Being, however, unlawfully detained in prison, he contrived to escape, got to Rome, and found great favour with the Pope, c

Nicholas V., at whose death he was named by the successor in St. Peter's chair captain of an expedition against the heathen. He is supposed to have been wounded in some combat, for he is known to have died in the island of Chios, and was buried in the church of the Cordeliers, a not unfit ending, according to the ideas of those days, for a merchant prince of France.

The Hotel Jacques Coeur, now converted into the Hotel de Ville of Bourges, is by no means the only relic of the domestic architecture of the Renaissance existing in the city. The Hotel de Lallemand also owes its origin to a family of financiers. In 1487 Bourges was nearly levelled to the ground by an awful fire; two-thirds of the city suffered, the trade of the place was almost burnt out, and never quite recovered. One Jean Lallemand, with his two sons, having thus lost the house in which they dwelt, and which must have been, like so many others, of sculptured wood, resolved to rebuild it in fair and fine stone. It was done, and that which they wrought is yet to be seen. In 1825, having hitherto been a private house, it was bought by the municipality, and the *S(eurs de la Sainte Famille* were installed therein. These sisters teach eight hundred little girls gratuitously. They show the Hotel to strangers for a trifling sum, which they devote to charity. The ceiling of the ancient oratory is worked in panels, each one differing in subject. The court is ornamented with medallions, several of which were spoilt in that fatal year, ",93." To it is uniformly referred all the Vandalism of Bourges, just as in England we lay it all to that unhappy Oliver Cromwell. The Hotel Cujas is so called from having been inhabited by a famous lawyer of that name, but it was not built by him. It dates from 1515, somewhere about the date of the earliest part of Hampton

Court. It is of brick, with stone ornaments, very graceful and beautiful. The great professor of law, Cujas, was an elder contemporary of our Shakspeare; he died in 1590. In his earlier life he accompanied the Duchesse de Berri to Turin. Possibly Portia may have profited by his lessons. See the historic charm and the romantic associations of these old houses!

Scattered through the steep and winding streets of Bourges are many other fine old dwellings, which yet have no special name. There is one in the Rue des Toiles, a second in the Rue St. Sulpice; and, were it possible to penetrate the secret of many another, what staircases, what vast apartments, what quaint sculpture, what elegant columns might we not discover! The town is a treasury of architectural art. Last year some gentlemen, supposed to be English, came and bargained greedily for the ceiling of the oratory of the Hotel Lallemand. They offered a mint of money for it,—perhaps they wanted to put it up in the Crystal Palace; but, *Bieu merci,* they were refused. The oratory was built three hundred years ago, for the honour of God and the delight of men,—not for a show, nor for reference in an architectural dictionary. It is *Berrichon;* in Bourges let it remain. We, who have Salisbury, Wells, Maplcstead, and many another glory of medieval art, need not go begging and stealing our neighbour's goods. If you wish to see the glorious treasures of Bourges, church and city, *come and look for them.* ON THE BRIDGE AT POISSY.
rjIHE nightingales were singing
At Poissy on the Seine, As I leant above the River,
Flooded high with summer rain. Dear is that royal River;
With ceaseless, noiseless flow, Past the grey towers of Paris
From the woods of Fontainebleau I
The nightingales were singing In the rosy sunset air;
The silver chimes were ringing,
"Christians, come to prayer!" And I thought the invitation
Utter d ever, eve and morn, Was the voice of good St. Louis

In the town where he was born!
As I leant above the River,
Musing softly all alone, The bells and birds together Seem'd blended into one;
The rapturous thrill of nature,
So soulless, yet so fair,
Borne up upon the winged chimes,
"Christians, come to prayer!"
Fair is the Seine at Poissy,
With its islets crown'd by trees, Fringed by spires of lofty poplars
Trembling in the summer breeze. Fair is the antique City,
And its Church as white as snow;
Built and bless'd by good St. Louis,
Built and bless'd so long ago!
Louis, being dead, yet liveth
By the waters of the Seine; Where he trod, his kingdom blossom'd; Where he built, his stones remain;
Where he knelt, his pious accents
Linger softly on the air.
Join, sweet birds, your invitation!
"Christians, come to prayer I" THE REVOLUTION AT TOURS.
rjp OURS is certainly the most charming town I have ever seen—Rome always excepted; and charming is perhaps hardly the word to apply to the metropolis of the Christian world. Here, in the centre of smiling Touraine, are such splendid churches, such picturesque old houses, such a wide, rolling river, such richly-wooded hills and luxuriant fields. The islands on the Loire are crowned with poplar spires; the gardens of the modern villas are bright with roses; and I saw a cherry-tree this morning, gorgeous with scarlet fruit in relief against the sky.
But if I inflict any more adjectives upon you, you will say that the florid Gothic of the fifteenth century has infected my style! And my thoughts have been running all day upon a subject of some gentle gravity, in which I am sure all will be interested—the tomb of St. Martin of Tours. I set out this morning to see an old house, said to be that of Tristan l'Hermite, the executioner of Louis XI. ,—rendered sufficiently familiar to us by the amiable portraiture of Sir Walter Scott. In the absence of authentic information, we may conclude that a profuse decoration of ropes carved in stone has

caused the house to be thus named. I found in a narrow street (Rue des Trois Pucelles) a tall, narrow, dirty, dilapidated brick house, its successive stories full of lodgers. The door and the windows are fringed with stone cut and carved. Fantastic stone animals crawl about the corners thereof. I liked it all the better for being old and dirty. One knows but too well the usual style of French " restorations how the poor old walls are made to glisten with soap and water; how a touch of paint is bestowed here, a touch of gilding there, and a coat of varnish everywhere; and how wandering antiquities are brought together from various quarters to take refuge in the "Musee." Nothing of the sort has happened here. The dirty old house stands in the dirty old street, appropriated to its original uses; and all its details can be investigated by the artist or the antiquary with a leisurely eye, without the help of a catalogue.

A curious brick tower, seventy feet high, is attached to the house; and the staircase is kept neat and clean, and is shut off from the rest of the dwelling. You ring for the *concierge*; you enter the court, and signify politely that you will give her a franc if she will take you to the top. The windows looking into the court are also ornamented, and over certain of them may be read the noble motto, "Assez aurons et peu vivrons." Under a vaulted recess is a stone well; and in the corner of the court is the door of the tower. Up and up we went; the bricks turning and twisting in extraordinary geometric curves. On the right-hand, in the wall, is a mysterious secret staircase, more like a chimney than anything else. The top emerges on the roof of the tower, and has been stopped up by the inhabitants of the house, who were probably afraid that the ghost of Tristan l'Hermite would continually climb up and down. This concealed passage has an ugly look, and I thrust my umbrella up from the bottom as far as it would go, and wondered how any human body could ascend that narrow channel. Once upon a time this secret stair descended into the cellars; but here also it has been closed; and the only opening is now into a sort of cupboard-recess in the main staircase. I have seen something like it on the rock of Cashel in Ireland, and both times the contrivance affected me with an indefinable sensation of fear. How awful to feel or fancy that while you were quietly walking up and down your family stairs, other creatures, with purposes unknown, were creeping about in the recesses of your walls, and might chance to drop out upon you in the middle of the night! Thin walls are apt to be damp, but at least they have this in their favour, that they cannot harbour secret stairs.

We reached the top of the tower, passing a small chamber where poet or artist might live most undisturbed. The top is covered over, but an open balustrade allows a view on all sides over Tours, whose roofs throng close up on every side. The sight of these ancient black roofs made me think of the revolution, and I asked the *concierge* if any of her family had suffered in the terrible storm which passed over the town. No, she said; none of her own family, but her mother had remembered it all; and the father of the late *propriitaire* of this very house had been guillotined. As she spoke, the *concierge* pointed to the high roof of a neighbouring church.

"That," she said, "is the Cannes. At least it was once the Cannes; it is now a parish church. The late *proprietaire's* father bought it to save it from destruction; and for this offence, this mere purchase, he was guillotined! His daughter has been dead only nine years."

"But the church was anyhow saved," said I; "the poor man was not guillotined for nothing."

Yes, the church was saved; and when, half an hour after, I entered its portal and walked softly up the pillared aisle, I remembered it had been saved at the cost of a devoted human life. If you ask me why the revolutionists did not pull it down when they guillotined the man, I can only answer that I imagine violent material destruction to be the work of a given moment of passion; that passed, even madmen would hesitate to pull down good stone walls, which might serve for a warehouse, as St. Andre at

Chartres; or a theatre, like St. Foy in the same town; or as St. Julien of Tours, which was long used as a *remise,* or coach-house for diligences! The two latter churches have of late years been redeemed, carefully restored, and reconsecrated.

To return to the top of the tower. The *concierge* showed me the direction of Marmoutier, where is the convent of the Sacre Coeur; concerning which I felt an eager curiosity and tender interest, for the sake of some English sisters. She showed me the tower of Plessis, the hills above St. Symphorien*;* and lastly, the two forlorn towers of St. Martin. I say forlorn, because the vast church which lay between them is absolutely gone, and its site covered with shabby streets, whose new houses contrast significantly with the hoary dwellings which once surrounded the cathedral.

"This one to the left," said she, "is the Tour de Charlemagne, and the other is the Tour de l'Horloge."

"And it is *gone,"* said I; "absolutely gone! What a horror! what a scandal! what an abominable shame!"

"Ah! que voulez-vous? c'est la revolution!" said the *concierge,* shrugging her shoulders.

"And have you done with them— your revolutions?" I asked; not unkindly, however.

She did not know; there were some folk who said *not,* —that it would not be unlikely to recur*;* and then as to the churches and religious establishments and the clergy, " C'est a recommencer!" It was the young people, she said, "la jeunesse corrompue*;"* and then everybody wanted to get above their neighbour. She did not know how it might be in other towns, but as to Tours!

In fact, my *concierge* did not take a cheerful view of the state of modern affairs, either as to social life or politics. We returned to the subject of the vast church of St. Martin. Twelve centuries it had stood; adorned with five towers; a centre of love and prayer. Now only those two solitary relics remained. But the bishop*;* ah, he was such a holy man! his very face was the face of a penitent, of a saint. The bishop sadly wanted to

rebuild the cathedral; and had a large sum of money collected for the purpose, but not enough. There was, however, always the tomb of St. Martin; and a great many people came from all round Tours to pray before it.

"How, the tomb?" I asked. "I thought you said the church was utterly destroyed and streets built over the site. My guide-book says nothing of the tomb."

She replied, " It was only discovered two years ago*;* long since your guide-book was published. It was discovered under a house; and the bishop has had a small chapel built over it; and it is there the people come to pray."

"And is it *really* the tomb of St. Martin *V* I asked, somewhat doubtfully; for the idea of finding a tomb under a house, seventy years after the church was destroyed, sounded very vague.

"Nay, I suppose so; they were very sure; and *il n'y a que lafoi qui sauvc."*

I felt sharply rebuked for my feeble attempt at historic criticism; and I told the *concierge* I would go and seek out the little chapel, and visit the tomb, about which the good bishop was so sure.

I left the house of Tristan l'Hermite, and plunged into the narrow twisted streets of Tours; past the flower-market; past the house with the groups of sculptured figures at every angle,—until I came to the immense solid dark Tour de Charlemagne, standing up like a single mast above the flood. I turned a corner, and there was the Tour de l'Horloge, its chimes ringing out the hour. It also rose massively from the houses at its feet; and the broken ornaments which were crusted into its surface clearly indicated the building which had been torn away from its flanks. The springing arch of the great entrance was yet visible; but a street ran right up what should have been the centre of the nave, one of the busiest streets of the town; and another street occupies the line of the transept. Who could believe that those noisy pavements cover the ground where countless thousands came to pray? for St. Martin of Tours was one of the four great places of pilgrimage of the world.

By dint of inquiry, I found out the temporary chapel spoken of by the *concierge,* and saw beneath it the block of ancient masonry in which the body of St. Martin had reposed; but in order to understand what I saw, I was obliged to read a book; and in order to make you understand likewise, I must give you a summary of its contents.

Ecclesiastical history tells us that St. Martin died on the Oth of November, in the year of grace 397,—not at Tours, but at a little town named Candes, situated at the junction of the rivers Loire and Vienne. The Poitevins and the Tourangeois each conceived they had a claim to the body of the saintly bishop; and the Tourangeois were successful, and brought the corpse to their own town. Tradition says that the vessel on which it was embarked floated up stream without sails or oars; that the trees on cither side burst into blossom, the sick recovered their health, and heavenly music was heard to accompany the boat until it arrived at Tours. The body was first deposited on the banks of the Loire, guarded by the clergy and the people, and was interred in a cemetery just outside the then existing town. Eleven years afterwards, St. Brice, his successor, built a chapel on the tomb, dedicated to St. Stephen; because at that time churches were dedicated to martyrs only.

Sixty-four years after the death of St. Martin, St. Perpetuus, at that time bishop, built a more spacious basilica, of which St. Gregory of Tours gives the description as the richest and most remarkable edifice then existing; and on the 4th of July, A.d. 473, the body was transferred to the new tomb. *Tins* is the tomb of which the masonry appears to be in authentic preservation at this day. I have said the *body* was transferred, but I should have said the bones; laid side by side, wrapped in a white stuff, and placed in a great alabaster vase, which was again enclosed in a chest, or *chasse,* of precious metal, of the shape of a coffin. The *chasse* was placed in the tomb, which was a little oblong construction, five or six feet long, and about three feet wide, which also was lined with metal

and fastened by a metal door. A marble stone lay upon the top, and above it the decorations of a rich altar; and hereon Mass was celebrated,—an honour, until that time, only accorded to the tombs of martyrs.

Now the basilica built by St. Perpetuus was destroyed by fire not very long after; but was rebuilt by Clotaire, and became increasingly sacred in the eyes of the Christian world. Kings came hither to ask for health or victory; queens, that they might prepare for death. It was visited by several Popes and holy bishops, and eminent personages were buried near the tomb. Under the direction of Alcuin a school was here established, which became the cradle of all the universities of France. The chapter held directly from the Pope, under the protection of the king. It was rich; it possessed the privilege of coining money; and could send armed men to battle in defence of its patrimony.

Therefore came the Normans, about the year 838, during the reign of Charles the Bold, and attacked the town; but the body of St. Martin being carried round the ramparts, they were struck with fear, and took to flight; after which the chapter, alarmed at the footing obtained by the Normans in other parts of the kingdom, removed the relics successively to Orleans, Chablis, and Auxerre, so that the tomb remained empty for about thirty-four years; and when the Tourangeois reclaimed their treasure, it cost a struggle, which resulted in actual warfare. The chapter of Tours was assisted by Ingelger, grandson of the Duke of Burgundy, who succeeded in bringing back the *chasse,* which was carried by noblemen, walking in the midst of the victorious troops.

We need not follow the vicissitudes of the church of St. Martin during the succeeding centuries. It suffered by fire again and again; but the tomb remained uninjured until 1562, when the Protestants pillaged the sacred edifice, and actually scattered the greater portion of the body of St. Martin. But in the following year the few remains rescued were restored to the tomb; and the spot in the neighbourhood of the clock-tow-

er, where the ashes of the different relics treasured in the cathedral had been cast, was surrounded by an iron grating, beside which pilgrims came to pray up to the date of the French Revolution. Then it was that the noble edifice, adorned by the munificent piety of ages, was finally ruined, the chapter dispersed, the apse demolished, the tomb ravished and destroyed; but the two great towers remained standing, and likewise the immense nave. A perspective drawing of the building while in this condition still exists. It remained thus until 1802, when the nave also was taken down; and only the towers now attest the glory of the ancient church and the Vandalism of its destroyers. The final act of demolition was consequent on a geometrical plan or map executed by the *commune* in 1801, which laid down streets and measured out houses over the whole site of the basilica. It was executed without the slightest opposition; and a crowd of mean-looking houses, strangely contrasting with the older piles of wood and stone in the vicinity, now encumber the consecrated ground. The Rue St. Martin runs nearly parallel with the ancient nave, and the Rue Descartes follows the line of the transept. The remainder of the site is covered by private buildings, only a fragment of the cloister remaining, excepting, of course, the towers.

Under these circumstances, anybody would have thought the pilgrimage to the Tomb of St. Martin, dear to all the country-side, was for the future a hopeless desire; but the piety of Tours refused to admit the idea. Under the Restoration, M. Jacquet-Delahay organized a subscription for the rebuilding of the basilica; but his project was abandoned, on account of what seemed at the time an insuperable objection. He had himself stated that the site of the tomb was traversed by the public way. Nevertheless, the popular devotion of St. Martin began to recover life and

D vigour, and pilgrimages were multiplied to the different places rendered memorable in his earthly career,—to Marmoutier, where he lived during his episcopate; to Candes, where he died;

to Liguge, where he founded the first Gaulish monastery. Also researches were made both in France and England for such maps or plans as might enable the exact proportions of the old church to be ascertained; and by means of the one made in 1802, mentioned above, and which was discovered in the archives of the prefecture, the exact position of the tomb itself was fixed upon; and it was proved that, contrary to the general opinion, this spot was *not* under the public way, but covered by one or more small houses.

In 1854, Cardinal Morlot, then Archbishop of Tours, had favoured the establishment of a pious association for giving clothes to the poor. It was called the *(Euvre de St. Martin,* and was identical with the "St. Martin's Charity" of an English village; both alike created in memory of the Saint having divided his cloak with the beggar. A member of the commission, deeply interested in the discovery of the site of the tomb, bought, in November, 1857, the houses supposed to cover the spot, but did not enter on actual possession until three years later.

On the 2nd of October, I860, the very day when the house actually came into the purchaser's hands, the commission began their excavations in the cellar, and found, as they expected, part of the old foundations of the choir. The house covered the site of the high altar of the basilica, and of a large part of the chapter in the rear, which had been called "Le Repos de Saint Martin." The arrangement must have been similar to that of the chapel of St. Edward the Confessor, in Westminster Abbey, or of St. Alban, in the church of the town which bears his name.

But the tomb itself could not be found. It was evidently beyond the limits of the cellar-wall—in that of the neighbouring house; and the works were suspended until possession could be obtained of that also; a small chapel being arranged in one of the upper rooms of the firstmentioned dwelling; where, on the 12th of November, the Archbishop of Tours, assisted by a large number of the local clergy, celebrated

Mass once more, after a lapse of seventy years from the destruction of the ancient altar. For the succeeding seven days Masses were celebrated almost without cessation, and the small chapel and the cellar were constantly full of people. A large red cross was traced on the wall of the latter, opposite to where the tomb was supposed to be; and a little lamp, hung from the ceiling, was kept burning day and night. A month later, the commission were enabled to excavate under the adjoining house,— the works being skilfully directed by an architect,—and before evening the continuation of the foundations of the choir were laid bare, and, crossed and somewhat injured by a thick wall of modern date, appeared a small oblong enclosure of stone, something between a coffin and a box. It showed signs of having once been arched over, and there was every probability that it was the sepulchre where the bones of St. Martin had once reposed. It was now eleven o'clock at night; hour after hour had passed in slow and careful search amidst the confused masses of ancient and modern foundations; and more than thirty persons were waiting in the outer cellar, communicating with the other only by a hole in the wall. When those within called out that they had found the two low walls of what appeared to be the ancient sepulchre, a spontaneous burst of voices gave out the Magnificat, which was echoed from cellar to cellar. On the following day the Archaeological Society of Touraine, represented by its president, its secretary, and various other members, visited the excavations, and decided that there was no doubt of their successful termination. A lecture had been given by M. Lambron de Lignier, a month previously, *apropos* of a paper, drawn up in 686, which had been found in the archives of Tours. This paper described the sepulchre of St. Martin as a small vaulted *cavcau,* of very white stone, 2 feet wide, 4 feet high, and 0 feet long, placed parallel to the direction of the church, and immediately underneath the hinder part of the Chapelle de Eepos. All these particulars correspond to the aspect and situa-

tion of the masonry discovered in December, 1860. The height of the pavement of the church was identified by the bases of various columns cleared in the vicinity, particularly of one of the four columns surrounding the tomb itself; and in some public works undertaken in the Rue St. Martin the famous well of the basilica was brought to light. Another singular discovery was that of a small furnace—apparently that which had been used by the Protestants who melted down the precious metals of the reliquaries, etc. All the foundations mentioned were identified with those on the plan or map of the ancient edifice; and it is as well proved as architectural evidence will allow, that the Tourangeois still possess the tomb in which St. Perpetuus laid the body of St. Martin. The only counter-argument arises from the numerous burnings and demolitions to which the upper church was subjected in the course of centuries; but it must be remembered that the tomb was solidly built under the level of the pavement, and the site, except in the outrages of 1562, regarded with scrupulous veneration and respect.

The present chapel is a low building of temporary construction, reached by a small door in the Rue Descartes. It occupies the site of the two houses mentioned above; and the outer wall of one of them remains in the Rue St. Martin, which runs at right angles to the Rue Descartes. The wooden floor of the chapel is on a level with the floor of the street; the tomb is sunk several feet below, under the altar, but is perfectly visible through a railing. Access to it is gained by descending a flight of steps, when a strange sight meets the eye: a space, about four feet in height, extends under the floor of the chapel; this is encumbered by heaps of masonry, and bases of columns; we are amidst the foundations of the basilica. On the side of the tomb there is sufficient height to allow of walking easily round it, the altar above being considerably raised. The curious, solid stonework is surrounded by a *grille.* It looks as old as anything in Rome; a strange, touching memento of our Christian forefathers, firmly fixed in the consecrated soil, while stately churches rose above it, and vanished away like the unsubstantial architecture of a dream.

I have only to add that the project of rebuilding the basilica has been embodied in various papers and plans, and especially in a *mandement* of the Archbishop's, dated November 6th, 1801. A subscription is open, and collections in aid are made in the churches; and Monseigneur Guibert says that if he can but accomplish it in his lifetime, he will exclaim with Simeon, "Lord, now lettest Thou Thy servant depart in peace." THE MONK OF MARMOUTIEBJ OB, THE LEGEND OF LIMERICK BELLS.

rjlHERE is a convent on the Alban hill, Round whose stone roots the gnarled olives Above are murmurs of the mountain rill,

And all the broad Campagna lies below; Where faint grey buildings and a shadowy dome Suggest the splendour of eternal Rome.

Hundreds of years ago these convent-walls Were reared by masons of the Gothic age:

The date is carved upon the lofty hills,

The story written on the illumined page.

What pains they took to make it strong and fair,

The tall bell-tower and sculptured porch declare.

When all the stones were placed, the windows stained, And the tall bell-tower finished to the crown,

One only want in this fair pile remained,

Whereat a cunning workman of the town, (The little town upon the Alban hill,)

Toiled day and night his purpose to fulfil.

Seven bells he made, of very rare devise,

With graven lilies twisted up and down;

Seven bells proportionate in differing size,

And full of melody from rim to crown;

So that when shaken by the wind alone,

They murmured with a soft iEolian tone.

These being placed within the great bell-tower,

And duly rung by pious skilful hand, Marked the due prayers of each recurring hour,

And sweetly mixed persuasion with command. Through the gnarled olive-trees the music wound, And miles of broad Campagna heard the sound.

And then the cunning workman put aside

His forge, his hammer, and the tools he used

To chase those lilies; his keen furnace died;

And all who asked for bells were hence refused.

With these his best, his last were also wrought,

And refuge in the convent-walls he sought.

There did he live, and there he hoped to die,

Hearing the wind among the cypress-trees

Hint unimagined music, and the sky

Throb full of chimes borne downwards by the breeze;

Whose undulations sweeping through the air

His art might claim as an embodied prayer.

But those were stormy days in Italy: Down came the spoiler from the uneasy North,

Swept the Campagna to the bounding sea,

Sacked pious homes and drove the inmates forth;

Whether a Norman or a German foe,

History is silent, and we do not know.

Brothers in faith were they; yet did not deem

The sacred precincts barred destroying hand.

Through those rich windows poured the whitened beam,

Forlorn the church and ruined altar stand.

As the sad monks went forth, that self-same hour

Saw empty silence in the great bell-tower.

The outcast brethren scattered far and wide;

Some by the Danube rested, some in Spain: On the green Loire the aged abbot died,

By whose loved feet one brother did remain,

Faithful in all his wanderings: it was he

Who cast and chased those bells in Italy.

He, dwelling at Marmoutier, by the tomb

Of his dear father, where the shining Loire

Flows down from Tours amidst the purple bloom Of meadow-flowers, some years of patience saw.

Those fringed isles (where poplars tremble still)

Swayed like the olives of the Alban hill.

The man was old, and reverend in his age;

And the "Great Monastery" held him dear. Stalwart and stern, as some old Roman sage

Subdued to Christ, he lived from year to year, Till his beard silvered, and tho fiery glow

Of his dark eye was overhung with snow.

And being trusted, as of prudent way,

They chose him for a message of import,

Which the " Great Monastery" would convey

To a good patron in an Irish court;

Who, by the Shannon, sought the means to found

St. Martin's offshoot on that distant ground.

The old Italian took his staff in hand,

And journeyed slowly from the green Touraine, Over the heather and salt-shining sand,

Until he saw the leaping-crested main,

Which, dashing round the Cape of Brittany,

Sweeps to the confines of the Irish Sea.

There he took ship, and thence with labouring sail

He crossed the waters, still a faint grey line

Rose in the Northern sky; so faint, so

pale,—
Only the heart that loves her would divine,
 In her dim welcome, all that fancy paints
Of the green glory of the Isle of Saints.

 Through the low banks, where Shannon meets the sea, Up the broad waters of the River King, (Then populous with a nation) journeyed he,
 Through that old Ireland which her poets sing;
 And the white vessel, breasting up the stream,
 Moved slowly, like a ship within a dream.

 When Limerick towers uprose before his gaze,
A sound of music floated in the air,—
 Music which held him in a fixed amaze,
 Whose silver tenderness was alien there;
 Notes full of murmurs of the Southern seas,
 And dusky olives swaying in the breeze.

 His chimes! the children of the great bell-tower,
Empty and silent now for many a year!
 He hears them ringing out the Vesper hour,
Owned in an instant by his loving oar.
 Kind angels stayed the spoiler's hasty hand,
 And watched their journeying over sea and land.

 The white-sailed boat moved slowly up the stream;
 The old man lay with folded hands at rest; The Shannon glistened in the sunset beam;
 The bells l'ang gently o'er its shining breast, Shaking out music from each lilied rim:
 It was a requiem which they rang for him!

 For when the boat was moored beside the quay,
He lay as children lie when lulled by song;
 But never more to waken. Tenderly
 They buried him wild-flowers and grass among.

Where on the Cross alights the wandering bird,
 And hour by hour the bells he loved are heard.

A WEDDING AT ST. DENIS.

 "YOU ask me, my dear, how our wedding went off. I have the satisfaction of replying, " In the best possible manner; the weather fine; the company well dressed." As for the more serious impressions of the day, you well know that they would be of the most effective kind. M. Amedee is a good young fellow; and the bride took with her to the altar all the best wishes of St. Denis. We went down by train, a whole party of us,—relatives, friends, children, and servants; the latter in their snowy caps and gay shawls. The wedding was announced to take place in the parishchurch, not at the *abbaye*. Hitherto I had always imagined that the two were one and the same. But no! The *abbaye* is the *abbaye*,—a noble and beautiful history of tbe age of St. Louis, bright and rich, as are all the monuments of bis piety. The parish-church is a small edifice approached by a broad flight of steps; and you may judge of my satisfaction when I found that it was attached to a house I have long desired to see,—that it was actually the chapel of the ancient Carmelite Convent, where lived and died the saintly Madame Louise, daughter of Louis XV. of France.

 It is impossible to say why this or that particular book specially moves this or that person. The Life of Madame Louise, accidentally borrowed some years ago, made upon me a deep and lasting impression. It tells a touching story: how, weary of the hollow gaieties of a profligate court, Madame Louise, then a little over thirty, sought, and with difficulty obtained, her royal father's permission to become a Carmelite nun. The pious daughter of a pious mother had long cherished this ardent desire; but it will easily be believed that the way was not smooth; at last, however, she carried her point, and made her profession in presence of her father and numerous members of the Court. The house was old; the community very

poor; but Madame Louise would accept of no favours. One amongst the others, at a time and in a circle where royalty was held in the most absolute reverence, the princess bore herself with a humility, a selfrenunciation, which would have been remarkable had she been nobody in the outer world, but which, in one accustomed from infancy to all the adulation of Versailles, showed a nature full of high courage and devotion. She was chosen mistress of the novices, and discharged her duties with affectionate zeal. Her old father used to come to see her now and then, and she had an influence over him which none of his other children possessed. He would come and sit in her cell, admitting himself by his own royal authority; and would jest with her in a fatherly fashion, half promising to repent of his sins. Last prosperous monarch of his race; poor, weak, handsome, generous Louis le Bien-aime! your good child loved you and prayed for you with unwearying piety; we also may hope and pray that this filial tenderness helped to draw down the pardon of an offended God. Madame Louise died a year or two before the breaking out of the Revolution—I think in 1789; died unconscious of the lamentable storm so soon to break over her country. She died blessing France, blessing her nephew the king, tenderly remembered in her convent; leaving a name holy and beautiful in the annals of religion. It was with lively pleasure that I heard the ceremony of yesterday was to be performed in the chapel endeared by her memory, built at her desire. It was with emotion that I entered the little door on the right-hand of the church, once evidently leading into the convent itself. The house is now a barrack; a sad desecration for the home of Madame Louise; but through the wide gate which faces the street, and at which two soldiers were loitering, I saw the arches of a little cloister; and from the small door at the side, by which entrance is also gained to the church, a wide staircase ascends to a room which is separated from the sacred building by immense folding-doors. I thought of the king ascending those stairs; of his daughter who waited dutifully to receive him; of their deaths so utterly forgotten; of her tomb, of which the *maire* told me there is no certain trace; of the utter oblivion in which France seems to hold her race; of her great-greatnephew spending melancholy days at Frohsdorf; of the many desecrations of which this one desecration is the type, —my heart was full of these things while I waited in the chapel for the bridal party, whom perhaps you will think I neglect too long.

The great doors at the top of the steps are thrown open,— a few friends wait for them on either side, and at last they come. The pretty, gracious bride in her white robe, crowned with orange blossom, is led by an old man with white hair, not her father; for, alas! she is wholly an orphan,—has neither parents nor grandparents. And then "le Monsieur de Mademoiselle," as her little pupils called M. Amedee during the time of the betrothal. Monsieur gives his arm to his aunt, a woman enjoying " une haute consideration " in the literary and benevolent world. Then come the little cousins and the sisters of M. Amedee,—he too is an orphan; then the crowd of friends. M. le Cure stands at the altar; he knows the bride from her childhood, and prepared her for her *premiere communion.* M. Amedee and Mademoiselle Lucile stand meekly before him; the good aunt takes up her post at the right-hand. We are all ranged behind them; but, alas! two immensely fat *messieurs* range themselves exactly between me and the bride; I have, however, a good view of M. Amedee and M. le Cure. The priest joins their hands; he performs the short marriage-service; the two are made one; and it is the moment for the *petit diseours* to be addressed to the married pair. We all sit down; the two fat *messieurs* plump heavily into their chairs, and I strain my ears to catch the purport of the sermon, which I imagine will be an abstract discourse upon the duties of the marriagestate. But it proves to be no such thing. M. le Cure *connait son monde;* and he improves the occasion with an eloquent earnestness which brings tears into the eyes of his hearers. After urging upon the young couple that they should remember in all things the God who had blessed their union, he says to M. Amedee, "You, 0 young man,—you who have been educated in a virtuous home, who belong to a family distinguished among others for its excellent reputation,—it is for you now to create for yourself a centre of similar influence." (M. le Cure here alludes to the good aunt, who had served as a mother to M. Amedee.) "It is for you to cherish all holy sentiments, all innocent and intellectual resources. I confide to you this day a young girl whom I regard as one of my children; cherish her; be to her a good husband." To the bride he says, "You come to the altar not unknown nor unrespected. To you the parents of St. Denis confide their little children" (she is

K mistress at the *salle d'asile);* "you have proved how well you merit their confidence, and they follow you this day to the altar with devout good wishes. You now enter a new sphere of duty; and I feel confident that you will exhibit the virtues of a Christian wife." Thus said M. lo Cure, at much greater length, in his elegant and expressive French. My neighbour cried, and I cried, and the good aunt cried; and I verily believe the young couple must have cried likewise; but I could only see the back of M. Amedee's head, meekly bent to receive the parental admonition. It was a beautiful and appropriate discourse, followed by the *mcsse tie manage;* after which a few moments were spent in prayer for the future life of the young people, and wo dispersed from the church to reunite at the *salle d'asile.*

This building, once a chapel nestled in the shadow of the *abba ye,* still retains traces of its ecclesiastical origin; the shape of the nave can be discerned on the outside, and within is a large room with a rounded end, now used as a play-room for the children. Here was laid out the weddingbreakfast, for fifty people, on a long, narrow table, twentyfive on each side. The bride took her station in the centre of one side, opposite to the bridegroom, who seated himself upon the other; and next to him was placed the good aunt. The *maire* of St. Denis, a burly, elderly gentleman, with white hair and bright, dark eyes, supported the bride. The half-dozen children and one or two *bonnes* were at a round table in the corner.

Then we began; -poUvje, roast veal, fish, vegetables, quantities of *vin ordinaire,* winding up with Bordeaux and champagne. The children had their full share of good things sent to their round table; every body laughed, talked, ate, and drank; and we wound up a two hours' repast with a violent clinking of glasses in every direction; all the guests, armed with their glasses, assaulted the bride, who clinked with everybody. The good aunt kissed M. Amedee tenderly on both cheeks, as if he had been a big baby. The universal *effusion* was something touching to behold.

People then began to think of returning home; but it was discovered that the stranger lady had never seen the *abbaijc,* whose great bell was booming right above our heads. We were assured that it was no use attempting anything of the sort; that the famous church had been under restoration for three years, and would be so for two years more; that the tombs were boarded up; that the effigies were temporary placed in the crypt, etc. etc. These difficulties were, however, graciously solved by the burly *maire* with the bright eyes, who offered to take us into the *abbaye* himself, and let us see everything in its present state, in spite of the workmen and the boards. So about twenty of us accompanied him into the vast building, which looked much as it must have done at the original building thereof. We walked round the numerous chapels of the choir; admired the painted columns, glistening with gilding and colour, and the rich stone carvings of tho altars, likewise tinted with many hues. We saw the fretted tomb of Dagobert, desecrated at the Revolution, when he and his queen, Nanthilde, were found lying together, enveloped in silk. Dagobert was buried A.d. 580, in the first chapel built on the spot; and his tomb was of course preserved by St. Louis in his reconstructions. The great sculptured monument of Louis XII., with its bas-reliefs representing the wars of the French in Italy and the king's entrance into Genoa, was covered up with an immense white cloth, of which a corner was lifted for our edification. The marble tomb of Francis I. was, however, fully visible; and several recumbent kings of the earlier dynasty, with straight figures and long noses, occupied the centre of the *ahbaye.* Those had been *scraped* at the Revolution, for the sake of the gilding, and were now in a painful state of whiteness and apparent newness; but, for all that, they were many a hundred years old.

Then we descended into the crypt, where was a strange population of monumental kings, all placed here temporarily until their proper sites in the upper church should be ready for them. There was Louis XL with his peculiar hat, and Louis XIV. with his streaming wig, and an endless scries of Charleses and Louises, and Jeannes and Marguerites,—queens in stiff petticoats, kings in strange oldworld coronets,— Marie Antoinette kneeling in her bridal costume, Louis XVI. ditto in his ample robes of state. The chapels of the crypt were crowded witli these mute effigies; and our footsteps seemed too many, and our voices too loud.

Lastly, the guide took us to a sort of circular vault, having gratings in the wall opposite to each other. The guide bade us stand at one of these while he went round outside to the other, and, placing his torch close to the bars, threw a gleam of strong light within. And we saw seven or eight coffins on trestles; two tiny ones of little children. Here lie the few Bourbons whom the ruthless hand of desecration or the sad leagues of exile have permitted to lie at St. Denis. Here are Louis XVI. and Marie Antoinette, whose remains were restored by a faithful royalist to their daughter the Duchesse d'Angouleme. Here are the Due de Berri and his two children, the Prince de Conde, the Due de Bourbon, and Madame Victoire Elisabeth de France, daughter of Louis XV., sister to Madame Louise. Here also are the coffins of Marie Lezinska (her mother), and of an old king and queen of centuries ago, whose tombs by some chance escaped the ravages of 1793. Here lies also Louis XVIII. Charles X. died in exile. Henri Cinq—who knows where *his* corpse will repose?

A far deeper melancholy than that of death lingered for me in this crypt of St. Denis. We left the dim and silent vault, and entered the cell where Napoleon, transferred from the Invalides, is one day to lie; but I cannot feel as if his rightful place could ever be among these kings of France of the olden time. I do not love this mixture of incongruous traditions. I am glad he is not there as yet. Let us leave them alone in their glory,—that glory of tradition which, even as regards effective authority, supplies many defects of character, many faults of government. For these were really the *fleurs de lys* rooted in the soil of the land.

Let us return to the *saile d'asile,* where M. and Madame Amedee are waiting to hid their friends adieu. The bride has distributed her bouquet to eager claimants; the children are standing on tiptoe to admire the bridal presents, particularly the sugar-basin with its silver handle. The old *bonne,* who has known M. Amedee from boyhood, is cryiug her eyes out from fatigue and excitement, and has to be consoled in a corner by a torrent of caresses and a lively application of strong salts. Goodbye, M. Amedee; goodbye, Madame Amedee. We leave you to occupy your pretty rooms, disposed under the pointed roof of your strange old ecclesiastical abode. May all blessings attend you, now and for ever! and may you be the model couple of St. Denis!

THE MASSACRE OF AVIGNON. OBESPIERRE reigned in the Place de Greve; And in distant Avignon his word was doom, When a band of Royalists, piously brave,

Tender and full the chorus rang,— *A l'heure suprSme, Mere chine,* Oka Pro Nobis, *Sainte Marie!*

The maiden young, and the grandsire old, And the child, whose prayers were shortly told; And the Cure, walking side by side With the baron, whose name was his only pride; The noble dame and the serving-maid— Neither ashamed nor yet afraid,—

Were marched to the edge of their gaping tomb. As they went on their way they sang—

A wonderful sight they were that day, Singing still as they went their way,— *A Vheure suprSme, Mere clierie;* Ora Pro Nobis, *Salute Marie!*

One of their murderers, waiting nigh, Heard them singing as they went by. And smiled as he felt the edge of his blade, At the fulness of music their voices made. "We'll stop that melody soon," said he, "In spite of their calling on *Sainte Marie."* But one by one as those voices fell, The others kept up the chorus well,— *A Vheure supreme, Mire cherle,* Ora Pro Nobis, *Salute Marie!*

When all the victims to death had gone, And the last sweet music was hushed and done, When the pit was filled, with no stone to mark, And the murderers turned through the closing dark, One of them wiped his sharp knife clean, Strode over the soil where the grave had been, And hummed as he went, with an absent air Some notes just caught by his memory there,— *A Vheure supreme, Mere cherie,* Ora Pro Nobis, *Sainte Marie!*

And when the thought of that day grew dim. Those obstinate words still clung to him. He was a man who said no prayers, But his lips would fashion them unawares; They mixed with his dreams, and started up To check the curses bred in his cup; They wove him round in a viewless net

Of thoughts he could not, though fain,
forget,
As he still repeated, again and again,
The ghostly air and the ancient strain,—
A l'heure suprSme, Mere cherie,
Oea Peo Nobis, *Sainte Marie!*

Thirty years were counted and o'er;
The lilies of France bloomed out once
more;
The grapes which hung on the vines
were ripe,
Like the penitent man on the threshold
of life;
When the Angel of Death with healing
came
For one who in Lyons had borne no
name
But " Le Frere d'Avignon" for many a
day;
Who living and dying would hourly say
('Twas on his lip as he passed away),—
A l'heure'supreme, Mere cherie,
Ora Peo N0B13, *Sainte Marie!*

SUMMER DAYS AT CHARTRES.

HY need one remain in Paris during
these hot dusty
days, overwhelmed with the *distrac-
tions du monde,* while so many beautiful spots, almost unknown to the English, are so easily to be reached? Who
would not rather wish to be strolling by
the high ramparts, or across the grey
bridges, and under the trim lime-trees
of one of the inexpressibly beautiful old
country towns of France? Who dares to
say that Paris is the centre of all attraction, when the exquisitely graceful architecture of medieval times, and the
fair green beauty of June, and the grand
traditions of the past, await one on
every side? See! the map is studded
with historic names: Maintenon, Le
Mans, Chartres. I never actually knew
anybody who had been at Chartres,
though everybody agrees that the cathedral is one of the finest in the world.

Chartres then let it be; but one cannot
now mount the *banquette* of a diligence,
and leaving Paris at early morn, travel
for hours through those richly-sown
arable plains till twin towers appear on
the horizon. Out by the Versailles railway we must go, and presently pass
Rambouillet, in whose royal *chateau,*
lived, for the greater part of his long

life, the sainted Due de Penthievre,
grandson, by the barsinister, of Louis
XIV., and grandsire, by the mother's
side, of Louis Philippe. Rambouillet, inhabited for two generations by this qua-
si-royal stock, was reclaimed by Louis
XVI.; and the aged Due removed to Ver-
non, on the Seine, taking with him nine
coffins,—those of his parents (Comte
and Comtesse de Toulouse), of his wife,
and six children; one of whom was the
Prince de Lamballe, husband of the
beloved friend of Marie Antoinette. These coffins, together with the Due's
own, were rifled in the Revolution, and
the contents thrown into a fosse. In
1816, when the mother of Louis
Philippe returned from exile, all she
could do was to raise a memorial over
the spot. What a subject for a picture
would be the removal of those nine
coffins leaving Rambouillet by torchlight! and how touching the old man's
desire that these sad remains of a once
happy home should go with him whith-
ersoever he himself did go to end his
days! Vain was the hope that he and
his might sleep together in honoured repose. Together they mingle with the
common earth,—nay, not even all together; for the fair features and graceful
form of Marie Therese de Lamballe,
found (so far as can be known) a last
rest in a graveyard on the south side of
Paris, carried thither in one of those ter-
rific dead-carts which slowly toiled up
the steep, narrow Rue St. Jacques after the "days of September." One who
walked there in the morning sunshine of
that fatal autumn, saw the row of carts
as they came onwards bearing their
ghastly freight. From one pitiful heap
protruded a fair white foot,—*un pied
defemme!* "Perhaps," says her biograph-
er, "that of Madame de Lamballe!"

But we must leave Rambouillet; the
train bears us on to Maintenon; the
chateau of which was given by Louis
le Grand to Franchise d'Aubigne, when
he married her and made her Marquise
de Maintenon, famous for all time. The
marriage is said to have taken place in
the castle chapel, and to have been celebrated by Pere la Chaise. Ere the mind
ceases to recall the gentle gravity and

possible dullness of those closing years
of the great man's domestic state, Ave
see the "twin towers" of Chartres rise
above the green horizon, richly gilded
by the setting sun. Nevertheless, it is a
mistake to call them twin towers, for, on
approaching the town, one is seen to be
worked and fretted and pinnacled, the
other severely plain. No more beautiful sunset-glow than shone that evening
over the ancient city ever greeted a traveller's eyes; it transfigured the mighty
pile of the church, and was cast back
from tower and gable and high-pitched
roof. The inhabitants walked in the
midst, radiant figures in a radiant world
of light. But before the hotel was
reached and appropriated, the sun had
sunk below the fields of corn; and before I made my way through a knot of
intricate streets to the cathedral, a heavy
twilight had descended on the town. A
heavy twilight! No better words can be
chosen! Not the evening glow,— that
was fading sombrely in the west; not
the black depth nor the starry splendour
of the summer night; but a wrapping
veil of twilight, which fell over the huge
cathedral with its closed doors, over the
narrow streets whose footways were
hidden under the projecting storeys of
the gable-ended houses. There was not
a sound in those dim streets, though the
great clock had not struck nine of the
summer eve. There was hardly a passer-
by. Chartres had retired to rest; or were
there any but ghosts inhabiting its antique dwellings? Ghosts that would peer
out as one stole past those barred windows, ready perhaps to troop to midnight mass of their own. The space
around the cathedral is narrow; and
from a rope flung across from its wall
to a neighbouring house depended a
lanterns, its dim oil-flame just marking
a point in the diffusive shadow. I
walked all round the vast edifice, which
looked of incredible size in that uncertain atmosphere, and ascended the great
steps on either side, leading up to broad
portals, fit to be flung open for the
solemn entry of a king and his people;
seeking whether haply some small door
might be found yet unlatched which
would admit me into the inner shrine.

But all was closed for the night. The statues of royal saints grouped about the west portal,— the "Porte Royale,"— looked down with calm Byzantine faces; the Prophets, and the Elders of the Apocalypse, and nil the great and glorious company which do inhabit the outer walls of Chartres cathedral, kept a stern, impassive guard that night. The church was as dark and silent as those wonderful streets; the *lanteme* was the only sign of human life; and that might have been believed to have been a mystic and self-supporting lamp, burning for ever before the vast tabernacle. I felt as if suddenly plunged *en plein moyen age.* Was it possible that here too the Revolution had passed with its swift and terrible wing?

Seen by daylight, Chartres is also strangely antique; these provincial towns of France are a hundred years older than any of our own. *We* date at furthest from the red brick of the Tudors; *they* from the carved stone of the date of our last invading Plantagenets. The streets of Chartres are steep, and break into frequent steps. No carriage can pass up or down; the laborious peasant women, with their white caps, emerge from the shadow into the sunshine, brilliant points of light. Green trees overhang the walled gardens; in one luxuriant *plaisaunce,* on the brow of the hill, immediately behind the cathedral, a party of young priests employ their recreation in a game of bowls. A *boulevard* extends over the site of the ancient ramparts, but the Eure creeps quietly beside, overhung with quaint half-ruined buildings of uncertain date; and yonder rises a ruined church, of which the remaining portion is turned into a warehouse. St. Andre was its name; founded more than seven hundred years ago. The choir was carried across the river; it is gone, but a crypt extends to the brink, or rather below the level. The round arches, the massive halfRomanesque architecture, tell of an almost immemorial time. Yellow waterlilies float upon the Eure; tall poplars tremble beside it. Over the steep slope of this side of the town rises the immense cathedral; and on every side lie the rich cornfields of La Beauce.

Over a queer little old bridge, and through an old, old gate, one passes from the *boulevard* to the crooked street; and here, immediately in the thoroughfare, stood on that June Sunday, a little altar, which a group of eager young people were decorating with white and pink calico; a priest gave the directions, and sundry little urchins sat on neighbouring doorsteps watching the preparations. It was not the first glimpse of white and pink calico, intermixed with flowers, which I had seen during my walk. In fact, one of the parishes was keeping the Octave of the *Fete Dleu,* by a procession,—" not like the *great* procession of M. l'Evcque," said the people; "*that* took half an hour to file past one; it was endless!" Nevertheless, this lesser ceremony was a beautiful sight in that sunshiny old Chartres. Wheja I had ascertained the hour, I retraced my steps to the *boulevard,* and waited by the principal *reposoir,* which was further decorated with a white image of the Blessed Virgin, and a profusion of lights and flowers. The procession came up to the music of a brass band, performed by striplings from sixteen to twenty. Then came troops of children, some of whose parents walked with them,—they being little toddling creatures, dressed in white, and so small as to be barely steady on their legs; there were the usual flock of townspeople, and a small congregation of gaily-dressed ladies, seated on chairs near the temporary altar; the whole scene lit up by the blazing sunshine, just mitigated by the faint, flickering shadow of the trees of the *boulevard.* It took about ten minutes for the procession to file up and group itself round the *reposoir;* and then the whole company fell on their knees, as if we had been in Italy or Spain,—indeed, the scene was southern in its beauty and romantic expression of devotion,—a scene which English Catholics can hardly look upon without being strangely moved. When all had passed away in the intricate streets of the town, I threaded my way to the church whence they had started and to which they would return. The small, quiet square in which it stands was ornamented with flowers, ingeniously sewn on to white sheets fastened up against the brick walls. This pretty device must be seen to be appreciated. Three banners hung from the windows of a house opposite to the open portal of the empty church. It was so hot and tranquil,—somehow it reminded one of Rome. A few people gradually collected, standing in groups about the square, half in sunshine, half in shadow; until at last the procession and its attendant crowd poured into the quiet precincts, filed up the centre of the church, and then arose the slow beat of the Gregorian Chant.

Such was the Chartres which presented itself that summer afternoon,—a city wearing its robes of antique beauty and picturesque devotion; but there is another and a very different Chartres existing in the associations of history, and which have left their visible trace. Petion was born here; and the hero of the town, doubly commemorated by an obelisk and a statue, is Marceau, the revolutionary general, who beat the Vendean army at Le Mans, and condensed much military glory into so short a span that he was " Soldat a 16 ans, general a 23; il mourut a 27." He was killed upon the borders of the Rhine; and only a month ago I found a half-tint engraving in an old portfolio—the funeral of Marceau—arms reversed, drooping feathers, melancholy officers on horseback.

"Honour to Marceau! o'er whose early tomb Tears, big tears, gush'd from the rough soldier's lid,

Lamenting, and yet envying such a doom,

Falling for France, whose rights he battled to resume.

Brief, brave, and glorious was his young career,—

His mourners were two hosts, his friends and foes;

F

And fitly may the stranger lingering here

Pray for his gallant spirit's bright repose; For he was Freedom's champion, one of those,

The few in number, who had not o'erstept
The charter to chastise which she bestows
On such as wield her weapons; he had kept
The whiteness of his soul, and thus men o'er him wept."

Had he lived, one is tempted to ask, might not the career of Napoleon himself have been warped from its aim of empire? A statue to Marceau in the town where Henry IV. was crowned King of France about two hundred years before,—what a gulf lies between! a gulf into which went down the traditions of a thousand years.

This Sunday evening I lingered in the cathedral till the last gleam died through the marvellous windows of thirteenth-century glass; jewelled panes, under whose dim, religious light the lamps shine like glowworms. Many days might one spend in deciphering their stories; many days in learning to know the manifold beauty of the glorious temple. What can the casual traveller acquire, beyond that deep, ineffaceable impression, made equally upon the imagination by the mountain, and the sky at midnight, by

"The leaves of the illimitable forest;
The waves of the unfathomable sea."

The next day, being bound for Tours, an hour's delay at Le Mans gave just time for a glimpse of the upper town, where is to be seen a group of architecture, close under the cathedral walls, not even mentioned in the guide-book, named by passers-by simply "un chateau," but whose profusion of peaked turrets and black, cobwebby, ghostful aspects, would have sent a thrill through the heart of Mrs. Radclyffe. It was inhabited too; not set apart as a museum, nor kept up as a trophy by any long-descended family. Naturally, and by the slow transitions of time, it seemed to have become the dwelling of the poorest of the poor. Without exception, it was the "oldest inhabitant" even among old French houses, and affected the eye like some forlorn centenarian among human beings, left standing amidst the rejoicing

strength of a new generation. In the cathedral is a monumental effigy of Berengaria, wife of Richard Coeurde-Lion, the beautiful golden-haired woman whom Scott has called to life in his 'Tales of the Crusaders.' The effigy is stiff, straight, formal, like one of the quaint figures in St. Denis'; the vision evoked by the poet, how radiant and glowing! I wondered if the two Berengarias typified the reality of that medieval past and the picture which we make of it for ourselves! Coming away from the cathedral, the traveller bound for the railway crosses that great open square where the Royalists and the Republican troops under Marceau fought desperately; the former, with their leader, Larochejacquelin, were expelled with fearful slaughter. By order of the Commissioners of the Convention, 10,000 persons, many of them defenceless women and children, were massacred for adhering to the dynasty and the faith under which France grew to be great among the nations. The memory of these things is sad and awful as one passes through the somewhat sleepy-looking streets of Le Mans. It is so short a time since; men are now living who may remember it, though the vastness of the tragedy seems to make it a tiling of the remote past. Are those contending passions truly laid to rest? Is the dream of a free and glorious republic yet cherished in the heart of the French "man of the people"? Do loyal bosoms yet beat tenderly for the exile who keeps no kingly state on the borders of the Adriatic,—the one white blossom of the Fleur-de-lys?"

The other town jotted down in the note-book is Blois; and Blois, though not a large place, should be taken in a leisurely manner. That great gloomy *chdteau,* that terraced garden of the Eveche, require thoughtful footsteps to explore the poetry of their sites. From the garden is to be seen a long panorama of the Loire. In the *chateau* inhabit the memories of a fearful past. A good spyglass ought to show Chambord from the former spot. The " Versailles of Touraine" gives his only acknowledged title to Henri Cinq. It was purchased

for him by public subscription. What a commentary on the Revolution!—a royal palace, built by Francis I., and occupied by Louis XIV., bought by subscription for the descendant who has hardly where to lay his head. He "has been confirmed in his possession, though the Bourbons have forfeited other estates in France, by the decision of the French law courts." It was purchased from the widow of Marshal Berthier, to whom it had been presented by Napoleon, and thus enters into a different category to that of the inherited estates. The rental is about £3000 a year, and was for some time expended by the Comte de Chambord on a restoration of the *chateau;* but for him its only charm can be the dear delight of possessing a hold on his ancestral France; for he cannot reside on his own land, and no son of his exists, within whose future might lie the real heirship of the fair domain.

The great, gloomy pile of the Chateau de Blois is full of historical associations of Catherine de Medicis; and her chamber, lined with suspicious and suggestive little cupboards, is shown to the traveller, together with the suite of rooms in one of which the Due de Guise was murdered. There is something in the rich, fantastic architecture which adds greater horror to the scene; most of our English tragedies were consummated in barbarous donjons, in old feudal castles; we were less refined and luxurious than Italy and France in the Middle Ages; *they* had blazoned ceilings and deep oriel windows, and twisted pillars, and a thousand interior elegancies of domestic life, which yet remain visible in the silent grandeur of these old *chateaux,* and are nevertheless streaked with blood, heavy with the vapour of poison, haunted with cruel crime. When one considers these things, one can half forgive Gaston d'Orleans, who passed here the last eight years of his life, and occupied himself in pulling down one side of the beautiful building, and re-erecting it in the villainous taste of the seventeenth century; had he not died when he did, it is probable that the whole would have been sacrificed. He is buried in a neighbouring church, and so is his daughter—that strange compound of passion and vanity and sad misfortune, "La grande Mademoiselle."

One might wander thus, note-book in hand, through the whole valley of the Loire. Touraine, the garden of France, is confessedly richer than almost any other province in its historical monuments; and there is a singular pleasure in referring to written reminiscences made amidst scenes like these, and in reviving once more the impressions made by their reposeful beauty and suggestive traditions. May these few touches refresh the traveller's memory, and serve to inspire the untravelled with a wish to visit one of those fair provinces whose names, rich with the associations of centuries, may indeed be banished from the map of modern Europe, but must ever live in history and in song!

FONTAINEBLEAU.

I walked in the grass-green alleys
Where fringes of beech-trees grow, I
thought of the close-cut lindens, And
the fishes of Fontainebleau,
The lazy fins of the old grey carp,
Almost too idle to eat their bread,
And the turreted roofs, so fine and
sharp,
Cutting into the blue sky overhead.
The suites of rooms both large and
small,
And the lofty gloom of St. Louis' Hall,
Mirror'd again in the shining floor;
And the thick walls pierced for the
crusted door,
With traceried panels and ponderous
lock,
Which opens heavily, shuts with shock,
If the hand unwarily lets it fall.
    The great square courts are still as
the grave, Once so joyous with hunting
horn,
When the princely hunter, eager and
brave,
Rode to the chase at the first of morn.
The grand old courts of Francis the
First,
Neither the ugliest nor the worst
Of that kingly race who hunted the deer
All day long in the forest wide,
Which stretches for miles on every side.
Music and feasting closed the day
When the king was tired with his hunt-

ing play,
And had chased the deer to his heart's
desire,
Where the sunshine glows, like soft
green fire,
Under the trees in the month of May.
    We were there in the month of May,
    When the quaint inn garden was
filled with flowers. Roses and lilies are
passed away, And I write in the dark
December hours.
But I will not believe (and a woman,
you know,
Will never believe against her will!)
That there ever is snow at Fontainebleau.
I fancied then, I will hold to it still,
That place of the ancient kings doth
wear
A sort of enchanted fairy-tale air;
And that roses blossom the whole year
through,
    And soft green sunshine glows on the
dew;
    That the breath of the forest is soft
and sweet;
    That dulcimers play in the open
street,
    And the people actually waltz to the
sound,
    Like the queer little folks that turn
round and round
    In the travelling organs you chance to
meet.
    At Fontainebleau, in the month of
May,
You just might fancy some amiable
gnome
    Or intelligent fairy had whisked you
away
A thousand miles from your northern
home,
And planted you safe on the hills near
Rome.
    It only wanted the olive-trees,
    And the purple breadth of the south-
ern seas,—
    Only a few little things of the kind,
    To make you doubly sure in your
mind.
    For there were the roses and there the
skies,
    And the wonderful brightness to fill
your eyes,
    And the people singing and dancing

away,
    As if constantly making a scene in a
play.
    And there was the moon when the
sun went down,
    And in silver and black she clothed
the town,
    As if half masqued for a holiday!
    Then the Royal Chapel of Fon-
tainebleau
    Is Roman quite in its taste, you know;
    Exceedingly white, and gold, and red,
    With a legion of cherubim overhead.
    But there the innermost heart is
moved,—
    Not by sculptured or painted *frise,*—
But by thoughts of a life perfumed with
prayer, Of a saintly woman who wor-
shipped there, The Wife of Louis the
Well-beloved,
    And Mother of Madame Louise.
    And then the Forest! What pen shall
paint
    The gates of brickwork, solid and
quaint,
    Which opened on it from every side;
    And the sweeping circles whose vis-
tas wide
    Narrow away to a point of space,
    Like the rays of a star from its central
place.
    Wherever you turn it is just the same,
    Whither you go or whence you came,
    To the right, to the left, behind, be-
fore,
    An ocean of trees for six leagues and
more.
    From the brow of the rocks (all pur-
ple and green,
    Or damply shining with silver sheen)
    You see what looks like a mystical
floor,
    A glorious level of green and grey,
    Till the uttermost distance melts
away,
    Where satyrs and fauns might nimbly
play,
    Swinging along by the tops of the
trees,
    Like dolphins out on the crested seas.
    And where the Forest is melting
away, And drops to the brink of the
winding Seine,
A vine-clad village, open and gay,
Tempted our feet,—but our quest was

vain.

We eagerly knocked,—but polite despair

Open'd the gate of the *porte-cochere,*

And a chorus of quadruped, white and brown,

Bark'd affirmative, "gone to town,"

With affable bursts of French *bow-wow;*

(As part of the family they knew how!)

So we gazed at the house through that *porte-cochere,*

With its tall new tower so straight and fair,

Its mouldings of brickwork quaint and free,

And under the date, a firm "R. B."

0 royal Forest of Fontainebleau, Be kind, be kind to this artist dear;

And if (which I don't believe!) you've snow,

Be silver-fretted, be crystal clear.

Be tender, O Spring, to her gentle kine,

To her lambs with coats so close and fine,

To the king of the herd, with horned brow,

Mademoiselle Rosa Bonheitr has established herself in a charming village on the outskirts of the Forest of Fontainebleau. Her house is old, but she has built on to it a handsome tower, of which we are told that the upper storey contains her studio, and the lower affords a home for various favourite animals.

To her rough-hair'd dogs, with their wise bow-

Nurture them, comfort them, give your best

To the family friends of your famous guest.

Thou, rose-clad Summer, temper your beams

With leaping fountains and gurgling streams.

Autumn, ripen your largest grapes,

Of richest colour and moulded shapes.

Rain, fall soft on her garden bower;

Sunshine, melt on the bricks of her tower;

Nature and Art, alike bestow

Blessing and beauty on Fontainebleau!

MEAUX AND EHEIMS.

TF one desires to see an old town, it is worth while to walk round it hither and thither until one seizes the typical aspects; to make the round of the walls, if there be any yet standing; to ascend the belfry, if modern improvements have left it accessible; to take a quiet stroll over the adjacent meadows; to climb the neighbouring hills. Then one is sure to be rewarded by a sudden vision of beauty never to be forgotten,—a picture complete in its unity, a portrait set in a fitting frame, an *expression* of the city henceforth indissolubly connected with its name in the imagination.

I have seen just such a picture of the cathedral city of Meaux, which may be painted by the brush of the travelling artist if he sits down upon an old stone just under the fence of M. Jacques Dumont's nursery garden, on the wooded hill due west of the town. M. Dumont's nursery is girdled by a lovely wood, which on the evening of the 24th of May, 1865, shone with a million raindrops in the yellow light of a setting sun. Whether to pursue the verdant paths, or whether to turn my back upon the sunset and sketch the town,—this question, important when one is starting by a morning train, divided my mind. I decided for the latter, and sat down upon the stone. At my feet was a deep valley, along which ran a canal and a railroad. The canal was nearest and on the higher level. I had crossed it by an old wooden bridge, accessible only for men and beasts; and before me had ridden a good-wife on a donkey, bound to one of the upper farms. Beyond was the iron rail, just where the town ramparts must formerly have been. Across the railroad was the arch of the town gate, and from it the small city rose steeply, surmounted by its cathedral—Bossuet's cathedral, literally the object of my pilgrimage. All round the other three sides of the city lay flat green meadows, green with the luxuriance of May, and tall poplars shot up on either hand, their clustering spires vying with the towers of the church, breaking through the red lines of the roofs, and carrying out that suggestion of peaceful aspiration so eminently characteristic of the architecture of a cathedral town. These poplar-fringed meadows are watered by the winding Marne—a pretty sylvan river, which turns numerous watermills, grinding corn and flour for the Paris market.

This mingled composition, wrought through ages by nature and art, might have challenged the pencil of De Wint. It is a subject which seems especially created for the walls of the old Water-colour Society. I am aware that this is putting the cart before the horse; but know not how better to realize Meaux to an untravelled reader, if such there be.

The rough pencil-sketch being jotted down, the tall front of the cathedral barely outlined, and poplar spires thrown in *ad libitum,* it was time to descend, for the yellow light was fading off the great western portal of St. Etienne, and soon the mist would surely be creeping over those flat meadows ere night fell.

The next morning, as we were bound to the church, the steep, narrow street was all alive with eager gossips standing on the doorsteps. We asked what was the matter. Nothing more than a wedding. M. Jules the draper was marrying Mdlle. Hermence, daughter of the butcher who lived next door. And we saw the guests come dandily down the street, the happy bridegroom driven thundering onwards in a coach and pair; and presently the young bride and her parents sally from their door, each and all dressed in excellent taste, and the whole affair got up with such care and neatness and absence of vulgarity, as impressed one very favourably as to the habits of the provincial middle class in France. We followed the party up to the church, the fine Gothic edifice of the twelfth and following centuries; and we witnessed the ceremony, followed by the *messe de mariage.* St. Etienne did not strike me as an especially beautiful cathedral; but then one is spoilt in the matter of French Gothic by the glories of Chartres and Rheims. But it looks large and ancient and quiet; it contains the grave and the pulpit of Bossuet, and the neighbouring Eveche is the selfsame house in which he lived. This is large and of many dates; the beautiful gardens extend to the rampart which still exists on the north. Some of the brickwork of the Eveche is of the time of Louis Onze, like that remaining fragment of Plessis les Tours; the stone vaults of the basement, once an open arcade, are much older. In the garden, away down a straight, embowered walk, is the pavilion where Bossuet loved to write. It has been restored; but parts of the walls are ancient, and the crumbling woodwork has been refitted exactly as it used to be. Here, too, are the trim yews, forming a close alley, where he paced up and down. The blooming flowers and the deep evergreens are just what they were two hundred years ago.

So little is known in England of that massive figure of Jacques Benign Bossuet, the Eagle of Meaux, as he was called in his lifetime! I have heard two more than competent English scholars speak of him, and one say to the other, with a shrug, "Oh, Bossuet was only an orator; a *great* orator certainly; but there was little else in him." But I could not help demurring to the verdict, thinking of the powerful square-headed man, younger contemporary of our own Cromwell, standing out in continental horizons as "a Father of the Church;" the man of whom Massillon said that he only needed to have been born in early ages to have been the illumination of councils, the soul of the assembled Fathers, to have dictated canons, and presided at Nicea and Ephesus. Truly a splendid eulogiuin, and with due allowance made for the favourable prejudice of Massillon, hardly to be hazarded to keen and critical French ears had its subject been only known as an ecclesiastical Demosthenes.

Bossuet was born at Dijon, in 1627, and early destined to the priesthood. He was only fifteen when he first went to Paris, arriving on the very day when Cardinal Richelieu was borne through the streets in the immense litter or rather portable chamber in which he had traversed France from Languedoc, borne by relays of eighteen guards. Sometimes the gates, sometimes the very walls of the different cities where he

lodged had to be taken down to allow him room to pass. Three months afterwards Bossuet saw Richelieu lying dead upon his bed of state. Deeply impressed by these scenes, he frequently referred to them in after-life. They formed an epoch whence he dated many things. He was ordained priest in 1652, and henceforth his name frequently appears as pronouncing public discourses; the one which chiefly concerns us is his funeral oration on our unhappy queen, Henrietta Maria, aunt of Louis XIV. It is worth while for an Englishman to read it, as showing the opinion a of a very competent Frenchman on our civil troubles of the seventeenth century, when they were yet but recent. This was in 1669. Scarcely seven months had elapsed when Bossuet was again called upon to lament the fearfully sudden death of our Princess Henrietta, the youngest daughter of Charles, and sister to that fair image of death which our Queen has erected in the church at Newport, near Carisbrooke, in the Isle of Wight. This poor Princess Henrietta, who had been in England visiting her brother, drank one afternoon a glass of chicory water, and was instantly struck with violent pain, to the utter confusion and dismay of the Court physician, who could do nothing. Henrietta asked again and again for Bossuet, who hurried to St. Cloud. Three hours after midnight she died, preserving her intellect to the end, and accepting from him all the last consolations of her faith. It was when preaching on this sad event that he struck grief into the hearts of his audience by that short and terrible expression, *"Madame est morte!"* repeating it as though it were hardly to be credited in that brilliant Court; and thence deducing his pious lessons. It would be worth while also to read this oration upon a daughter of England; she who was niece to that princess through whom our Queen inherits.

Not much longer would I detain my reader upon the career of the great Bossuet. How he was named preceptor to the Dauphin; how he became Bishop of Condom, and resigned his bishopric because he could not reconcile the two du-

ties; and how hard he worked to conduct the prince's education on the best plan,—all this may be seen in the story of his life. We also find him combating the king's successive passions for Mile, de la Valliere and Mme. de Montespan; the latter in 1675. It was in May, 1681, that he was nominated to the bishopric of Meaux; he was fiftyfive when he in the following year took possession of bhat house and garden still to be seen by the traveller. He lived there during the time of his troubles with Fenelon—Fenelon who is so exclusively the favourite of the English that they hardly recognize his great opponent. In the same pages are also to be found his opinions and his actions on the great Protestant controversy then distracting France, during which it will be seen that he did his best to influence the king to mildness, and never countenanced persecution. It was in August, 1703, that he fell dangerously ill at Versailles; it was at Paris, on the 12th of April, 1704, that he passed away to his rest, aged seventy-six years. His body lay awhile in the Church of Saint-Roch, then it was removed to Meaux, where he was buried in great love and honour, at the foot of the high altar, on the right-hand, or epistle side. His tomb was spared at the Revolution, and still reposes under that Gothic roof, around which the tall poplars cluster so picturesquely as one sits upon the hillside to the west of the episcopal city of Meaux.

From Meaux we were bound to Rheims, the city of coronations; and we bowled through the Champagne country, and past the magnificent residence of " La Veuve Cliquot," under whose able feminine rule the vine business flourished so well, (this lady, lately deceased, was reported to be the largest grower in France,) until we came to the clean, quaint, old-fashioned town, on whose outskirts civilization has set a railway, a boulevard, and a public park, which contrast oddly with the massive Roman gate standing up forlorn beneath this Northern sky.

Rheims, says the respectable voice of history, (which vóice is so exceedingly monotonous, unless you hear her discourse in the very localities,) was already a large city when taken by Julius Caesar. Bronze coins have been found of anteRoman era; the most important bore the device of three heads, all turned to the left, and the inscription Remo. The Conquerors built temples and palaces, triumphal arches, and a capitol. When the railway station was made in 1860, the workmen laid bare a magnificent mosaic floor. Then came the long middle-ages, Merovingians and Carlovingians, a chronicle of fighting and baptizing; here and there a saint or two—Jovinus, the Christian Consul, who was absent when Attila appeared before Rheims,—St. Niccixe, who was killed on the ramparts by that objectionable Him (406), and St. Remy, who was archbishop in the time of Clovis, and assisted the Queen Clotilde in her successful endeavours to induce the king to become a Christian. Later, church councils were held at Rheims, presided over by Popes; and one archbishop was raised to the Chair under the name of Sylvester VII. This was in 999. The instructed reader may further recall to his imagination the quarrels of the *bourgeoisie* with the clergy, from the twelfth to the fourteenth century, and the silencing of the same by the gradual pressure of royal power; the coronation of Charles VII. in the cathedral, under the auspices of Jeanne d'Arc; the struggles of the Ligue, when Rheims made great sacrifices for the Catholic side, and her defeat of the Spaniards under Louis XIV.

It is enough to mention these dates, just to show that the old city took her share in all the fortunes of France; and the modern traveller may be pardoned if he rolls into the railway station with only a general jumble of the facts in his head.

We put up in a roomy, middle-class inn in the Rue Large, built with arcades, something like the Rows at Chester,—a regular old French inn, upstairs and downstairs; two courts, and my bedroom looking into one; with a full view of the kitchen, the man-cook in a white cap, and two old women, whose existence seemed to be passed in shelling kidneybeans. And there, having no dust

of travel to shake off, we looked at a map; a nice, little, neat map of the town, with the public buildings marked in deepest black, and nsked ourselves what we had come to see. On my part, this was easily answered. I had come a long way to see all that remained, and which the imagination could reconstruct, of the medieval city. Look at the panoramic map, with towers, spires, and gable-ends, the encircling walls, and little conical towers with their nightcaps ou! To the left, you see the renowned cathedral, with the deep recesses of its triple portal, and to the right, the pointed spires of the Abbey Church of St. Remy. This splendid old edifice, dating its foundation from the beginning of the fourth century, and exhibiting in its architecture the traces of each successive year, was, at the Revolution, turned into a stable and exercisingground for horses! The rich works of art were broken up, and the treasure sent to the mint. The tomb of St. Remy, with its twelve statues, was also knocked to pieces. All this has now been restored with long care and pains; the north tower rebuilt, as likewise the rose window, and the saint's tomb recarved; such of the statues as were partially entire being again put up in their old places.

As for the rest of the town—all that mass of gable-ends, bristling with intermediate spires—there is not a square yard unbeautified to the imagination by some romantic or terriblo event. The fortifications stood entire until 1722, when the first gate was demolished, and replaced by a simple palisade. Presently the authorities began to plant promenades outside the walls, and having taken down a second gate, they built a new one in its place, through which Louis XV., returning from Flanders, made his entry into the town. Two others were destroyed at the coronation of Louis XVI.; and so, one by one, just as happened at our own Canterbury, the traces of medieval warfare disappeared; it is less than a hundred years now, since the Kentish farmers, complaining that the loads piled on their carts were knocked off by reason of the lowness of the arch, prevailed on the town authorities at

Canterbury to take down a magnificent old gate. For thirteen days did those "cruel men" pick and batter at the old masonry before they could abolish it.

As it is impossible in our limited space to touch upon half that Rheims contains of interest, we will take two periods of her history, both recent, and say a few words upon each; being, as they are, a curious contrast the one to the other. Firstly, then, the Revolution, which, as in so many of the provincial towns of France, brought its dismal tale of crime to swell the general calendar. Louis XVI., crowned here, as was each French monarch from age to age, touched the crown uneasily, as it was placed upon his broad, sloping brow, and said, "Elle me gene;" it was the opening word of the drama, which began here, as elsewhere, with amiable patriotism, loyal petitions to the throne, the foundation in 1791 of a "caisse patriotique," all whose notes enjoyed the best credit, and were scrupulously met. But the silver stream swelled to a roaring torrent, and in September, 1792, Rheims had its massacres, directed not, however, by a townsman, but by a Liegeois named Beaucourt, and some commissioners from Paris. The first victims belonged to the post-office; and, we may just observe, that a battalion of Federalists, partly composed of those same Marseillais who were called to Paris by Petion, had come into Rheims from Soissons on the night of the 1st, in company with the emissaries of Danton, who ferociously desired to get up massacres in the provincial towns, coincident with those of Paris. The first person arrested was a postman named Carton; he had been in bad odour with the people for a year and a half, because he had objected to the tearing down of the arms in one of the squares. He was now arrested under pretext of having neglected to leave certain newspapers at their address, and the same municipal officers who arrested him also placed sentinels at the door of M. Guerin, director of the post-office, and at that of his neighbour, M. Canelle de Villarzy, accusing them of having abstracted letters and parcels. The news having circulated through the town, a great crowd assembled before M. Guerin's door by seven o'clock in the morning, and seeing, or fancying they saw, sparks issuing from one of the chimneys, took it into their heads that M. Guerin was destroying papers inimical to the public weal, and furiously demanded entrance. During that day the house was under charge of two members of the municipality, and an official inspection was made, the result being a declaration that nothing had been found. But at eleven o'clock at night, on an alarm of fresh sparks having been seen, another visitation was made; and if the report can be trusted (where so evident a desire for bloodshed existed), burnt papers were found in the kitchen chimney, some even in process of destruction. Guerin and his female servant were forthwith arrested and put in prison; as also M. de Villarzy. From this moment all was a wild scene of confusion. The great square and its adjacent streets were filled by a vile mob, among whom mingled Federal soldiers and volunteers. Hoots and cries and reiterated demands for the blood of the prisoners spread terror throughout the town. The National Guard took up arms, as did the troops lodged in Rheims; but these latter were more than inclined to fraternize with the multitude. One hour after noon a fourth arrest took place,—that of a M. de Montrosier. His father-in-law M. Andrieux, who was one of the municipal officers, tried to save him, and the councils wavered. But Beaucourt was not apt for mercy, and set off to seek Montrosier himself, who followed "sur sa parole." But when they were about to mount the steps of the Hotel de Ville, Beaucourt turned round sharply and said, "Gueux, c'est en prison qu'il faut aller," and took Montrosier there himself. As he returned to the Hotel de Ville, fresh cries of " La tete de Guerin" were heard. "Mes amis," replied Beaucourt, "vous voulez du sang, vous en aurez." In another moment a beam was being raised hard by the post-office, on which, to hang the unhappy director. What need to particularize further? The authorities themselves favoured violence, and

would not listen to the National Guard, when they desired to attack the mob. The prison was forced, for Guerin was dragged out and massacred before he reached the spot where the rope awaited him. A sapper cut off his head with a hatchet, and it was borne through the town on a pike, then taken to the cathedral, where the electors of the department were gathered to name *deputes* to the National Convention. Other wretches fastened a cord to the garters of this first victim, and so dragged the headless body about the town; and finished by laying it before the house of a relative. The poor postman Carton shared the fate of his master. His head was carried about fastened to the end of a broomstick, and a farce enacted of forcing beer into the poor stiffened lips. M. de Montrosier, taken from prison under promise that he should be brought before the municipality, was wounded on the back by a blow from a sabre. He fell, was killed, and his head was taken to his own house, and would have been presented to his wife, had not a servant fortunately barred the door in time. The priests were the next to suffer; two *ah-bis* from the environs were brought in and massacred on the steps of the Hotel de Ville. Two others were seized, successively wounded, and thrown on to a pile of burning wood, on which they died. The next day l'Abbe Paquot, the cure of the parish of St. Jean, a man of sixty, and dean of all the cures of the town, was the first victim. The assassins came to his home at nine in the morning, headed by one Chateau, a weaver, and took him to the Hotel de Ville. They found him in his dressing-gown; but he got leave to change it for his *soutane;* and his arresters covered his white hair with the red cap of revolution. They tried to force him to take the famous constitutional oath; he refused; treated with personal violence, M. Paquot held firm. Some members of the municipality, who had come to make a vain endeavour to save him, read out to the murderers the law requiring the deportation of priests who refused the oath. They even begged hi in earnestly to take it; but the poor priest made answer, "Je

ne le puis. Si j'avais deux ames, j'en donnerais une pour vous; mais n'en ayant qu'une, je la garde pour mon Dieu." Hardly had he finished these words, when the assassins pushed him out of the room, killed him, cut his head off, separated his limbs one from the other, and conducted themselves with indescribable and untranslatable ferocity.

The next victim was the Abbe Suny; he was more than eighty years of age. Women cried out, in vain, that he might be spared, as did many of the municipal officers. He was done to death by a band of ruffians, headed by Chateau the weaver.

In this time of terror, one man only showed effectual courage in saving the innocent. A certain Madame Gonel, imprisoned as "suspecte," was threatened with death by the assassins who rushed to her cell; they were repulsed by Monsieur Hedouin de Pons Ludon, who was twice shot at by the brutal, drunken wretches, but succeeded in saving the lady.

Will it be credited that, on the night of the 4th-5th of September, the horrible fiends amused themselves by roasting the flesh of their victims? and—we need add no more! There is a certain satisfaction in winding up this portion of the story, by recounting that Chateau was sacrificed to the necessity of throwing the blame upon somebody. He was accused of having murdered the Abbe Suny, and brought before the civil authorities, who had remained passive during the previous horrors. Chateau naturally tried to defend himself by calling upon Beaucourt, the *Procureur de la Commune,* and threatening to tell all he knew in regard to the complicity of those in power. Beaucourt grew white with fear, and exclaimed, "Voila donc le sanctuaire des lois qui va encore etre ensanglante." But he recovered his equanimity when Chateau was dragged out of the hall and put to death upon the outside steps, to the cries of " Vive la Nation." The body was taken to the cornmarket and thrown into a burning pile; and his wife had a narrow escape of being converted into an involuntary Suttee. A detachment of the National Guard, aided by a company of Breton soldiers, were barely in time to save her from a vile mob, intermingled with Federalists and volunteers. One of them had got her by the neck, and was dragging her towards the fire. Capitaine Blin, fearful that in another moment he might be too late, ordered his men to fire upon the group of miscreants, and the miserable fellows straightway dropped the woman and took to their heels.

Nothing is more wonderful in all these stories of the Reign of Terror, both in Paris and the provinces, than the way in which the civil authorities appear to have yielded behind the scenes. Emissaries were doubtless sent from the metropolis to ferment the passions of the mob; but local elements fused only too readily with that which was foreign to the towns. Then, when a lingering sense of decency seemed to demand public notice of the atrocities, social vengeance fell upon some victim no worse than his judges, except that his right hand was perhaps the wettest. In 1795, others of the assassins were condemned to severe punishment or to the guillotine; but the Reign of Terror cannot be said to have ceased until 1796, for in March of that year the Representative Thunot condemned a nobleman and a priest to death, "pour fait d'emigration."

We will pursue these terrible themes no longer, but turn to the chief monument of Rheims—the mighty cathedral which has stood through all the strange vicissitudes of French history, but whose great office, that of witnessing the coronation of the kings of France, seems now at an end for ever. I sat on a stone in the irregular square which spreads itself before the great west front, and looked up at its thousand intricate carvings, by the light of a May moon, so brilliant that it might have been that of Italy. There was neither sound nor movement abroad, save the rare footstep of a late pedestrian, though the hour was only ten; and the sight was to me infinitely more touching than even that of Notre Dame de Paris. The procession of mighty men who had en-

tered through the centre arch of that triple portal were but the descendants of those crowned and anointed in earlier churches occupying the same site. Clovis was here sceptred; and here Louis le Debonnaire, Lothaire, Hugues Capet, and Saint Louis were made into kings. Saint Louis was the second monarch crowned in the present edifice, which was commenced about A.d. 1210, the preceding one having been destroyed by fire. His coronation took place on the 1st of December, 1226. Then comes the long romantic *role,*—Charles VII., indebted for his crown to Jacques Coeur and the Maid of Orleans, who here carried the standard of France; Louis XL, of unblessed memory; the amiable Louis XII.; the splendid Francois I., friend of Titian, and contemporary of two other great kings of England and Germany; then the fair, frail Medicean youths. Henry IV. was not crowned here; Rheims was too Catholic a city for the Huguenot prince,—the quarrels between them were long and many. But Henry's son, Louis XIII., was crowned and anointed at the ancient altar, and so was Louis le Grand, Louis le Bienaime, and the martyred " Capet," against whose name a brutal pen scored in the prison day-book, still to be seen in the archives of Paris, the coarsely significant word "raccourci." Then came the bloody torrent of trouble which I described in a previous page; and here it would seem as if the story of Rheims cathedral would fitly end. How could this town, in which priests were dragged from their knees and murdered in the public place, in which victims scarcely dead were thrown into piles of burning wood, in which all law and order and sanctity had been, for many days of 1793, disregarded; over which an army of Russians marched in 1814, and were followed the next day by the troops of Napoleon, violent engagements taking place, and more than four hundred cannon-balls being discharged against the fortifications, many of the balls and bombs pitching over into the streets, where mothers ran about distractingly, carrying their infants in their arms; how could this town, where Napoleon re-en-

tered victorious, lodging three days in the Rue de Vesle, during which he worked incessantly, wrote to " Joseph" at Paris, scolded the Abbe Macquart for having persuaded his old friend the Russian General Saint-Priest, to spare the town (" Napoleon lui reprocha des relations avec les etrangers!"), and finally quitted, having named prefects to enforce his authority; how could Rheims ever again comport itself like a loyal, respectable town of the *moyen dge,* and gather itself together to witness a royal coronation of a Capet? Yet so it did; and there is something almost ghostly in the idea—something sad and pathetically unreal.

It was at two o'clock of the afternoon, on Sunday the 29th of May, in the year 1825, that Charles X.—he who was Comte d'Artois in those days when the youthful group of grandchildren dwelt with Louis XV. at Versailles—came in his old age to be crowned the last king of France. Henceforth the land was to possess *un Roi des Franqaii,* a President, an Emperor,—and who knows what to follow? But the kings of France, that long, picturesque line of men whose story is the most romantic in the world, had unwittingly their last crowned descendant in the old man with the,'high head and hooked nose, who entered Rheims that day with sound of music and booming of the great bell of the cathedral. Splendid were the preparations which had been made to greet him. In the Archiepiscopal Palace one sees the handsome rooms—full of a certain magnificence, of the style of forty years ago—where he lodged for several days. The great church was lavishly adorned with all the treasures of religious art; and the vessels of gold plate used at High Mass and in the consecration are yet shown to all comers. The king held a grand review of all the troops camped about the gates of the city; he visited the civil and religious establishments, and created a fresh batch of *Chevaliers da Saint Esprit.* By his side were the few members of the royal family who had escaped the awful storm of the Revolution. They are to be seen in the historical picture of the coronation, which is now in the Musee de Versailles. Madame d'Angouleme was there, the daughter of Marie Antoinette; she who at the age of fifteen learnt the bereavement of her hearth by her waiting-maid bursting into sudden tears and saying, "Madame n'a pas-de parents." The young Due de Bordeaux was there, a child of tender years, the king's grandson, born after his father's assassination; and the child's mother, the Duchesse de Berri—she who had the spirit of a man to defend the royalty of France. And the family of Orleans were there, so soon to reign in Charles's place—so soon to find an equal fate in exile. And the peers of France were there—Montmorencies and Rohans and Noailles,—accompanied by the graceful women of each noble house, and all clad in the most gorgeous robes of state, and wreathed in smiles because the heavy days were passed, and their order was supreme once more. Then the head of the king was anointed with *la sainte ampoule,* the holy oil which the legend declares to have been brought by a snow-white dove from heaven, and given to St. Remy for the baptism of Clovis. And the singing of the chorister boys rose sweetly into the vaulted roof, as it had done in the days of Jeanne d'Arc, when she stood beside that high altar with u the Oriflamme in her hand; and *Bourdon,* the great bell in the tower, rang far and wide over the horizon. And the king was crowned and anointed, the tenth of his name and the thirty-ninth of his race.

But when the fetes were over, and the last of the glittering company had filed away through the gates of Eheims, its wonted calm fell upon the ancient town. The pageant had vanished as a dream, and its results were wellnigh as fleeting. The inauguration of a new era was at hand; the railway and the factory came and established themselves on the outskirts, full of bustle and mirth; and the streets in the centre became grassgrown and picturesque. No ioyal processions enliven their handsome outlines; and the burning sunshine alternates with the bright moonlight of May, bringing out the marvellous portal of

the cathedral into magic relief; but the traveller hears few footfalls at noon or nightfall, when

"The large sun slowly moving down
Flushes the chimneys of that town;
It is past the ringing hour,
There is silence in the tower;
Save that on a pinnacle
A robin sits and sings full well.
Hush!—at length for prayer they toll:
God receive the parted soul!"
BOURG LA REINE.

HROUGH these close-cut alleys Paced Gabrielle;
At her side, in royal pride,
Henri bon et bel.
All! my love across the sea,
Dost thou love me as well?
    On such an autumn night, Long years ago,
Fell the shadows on the meadows
Of the old chateau;
All along the gabled roof
    The moonlight lay like snow.
    Trembling with a world Of hope and fears,
She would wait by this old gate
Watching through her tears,
While he rode from Paris streets,
    Unguarded by his peers.
    He, as he came riding on,
    Knew full well Where she stood outside this wood;
    Many a song doth tell How she loved this knightly king, *La channante Gabrielle!*
    Clash and clang of swords Soon dies away;
Shrined apart in a people's heart
Love lives alway;
France will not forget this name,
Gabrielle d'Estrecs! SENS-SUR-YONNE.

Hdtel du Grand fecu. HEN I look out of my window across the inn-yard (which is shaped like a long horse-shoe), I see a white baby being carried about by a *bonne* in a frilled cap, and beyond him, over the curving roof of the horse-shoe, I see the great west front and towers of the cathedral rise like a huge fretted rock, golden in the light of the setting sun. These are respectively the youngest and the eldest of the *Sennonais.* I claim for St. Etienne de Sens the dignity of being the oldest inhab-

itant, for it was founded the year A. d. 270; the baby, on the other hand, is barely seven months in the world. The boy is baptized as Paul, the church is christened Stephen. Paul is dedicated to the Virgin, after a pretty fashion common to French mothers, and is clothed in white from his boots upwards. St. Etienne is built of great blocks of white stone, which age has darkened to a variety of soft greys and browns, except in the interior, where it shines like snow. Paul is a lively baby, keeping up a ceaseless demand upon the attention of bystanders. St. Etienne rings large bells and little bells from early dawn to falling eve. Lastly, St. Etienne is one of the noblest churches ever wrought by mortal man; but little innocent Paul is a " living temple, made without hands."

This hotel is kept by Paul's father and mother. When I walk along the corridors and look into the rooms, which are, some of them, very stately, I think the house must once have belonged to the *noblesse.* For instance, there is the chief bedroom, with two large windows, and folding-doors which open in the great saloon. A heavy beam runs across the ceiling, a high wainscot clothes the walls; in part of the room the panels rise to the ceding, notably over the fireplace, where a picture is inserted which represents a young man playing on a musical instrument to a young woman who sits under a tree. I think that this panelling was put up in the last century, and that the Arcadian scene was then incorporated. The building is much older than the art. Our best bedroom contains two large beds, draped with long curtains, red flowers on a brown-buff ground, and the walls are adorned with four allegorical portraits of the Seasons. Winter is a lady in a black dress, seated by a marble table, on which is a lighted brasier. In her hand she holds a small mask, and when I first looked at her I felt convinced it must be Madame de Sevigne. Such great people found Sens in the direct line with the south, then as now, and came posting down to sleep here, from Paris. On Wednesday, the 3rd of June, 1675, Madame de Sevigne writes to her daughter, Madame de

Grignan, who had left her after a long visit, "Je n'ai recu aucune de vos lettres depuis celle de Sens, et vous savez quelle envie je puis avoir d'apprendre des nouvelles de votre sante et de votre voyage; je suis tres-persuadee que vous m'avez e'crit: je ne me plains que des arrangements ou derangements de la poste." It is, however, probable that Madame de Grignan would have lodged in a convent, being *tres-Uee* with various high ecclesiastics, and herself the great-granddaughter, through her mother, of Ste. Francoise de Chantal. But it is more than likely that she had some sort of acquaintance with the family who then dwelt in this great hotel.

Indeed, the place is so full of associations that it affects me like a waking dream. I cannot quite realize that it is really the nineteenth century; and yet one had needs do so, for it is not thirty years since the mayor and municipal council deliberately pulled down the splendid old walls and picturesque town gates, which were literally of all ages, from the third century to the fifteenth.

I asked a townswoman one day why this peculiarly barbarous thing had been perpetrated. "Oh " quoth she, " on veut toujours etre a la mode I"

And this *mode* has been for Sens of so many divers fashions. If one lies awake musing in the darkness, one sees first the wide valley of the Yonne lying in the stillness of the primeval forest, and then the Gauls coming to take possession, and fixing here a populous city. Of their habitations no trace exists; but when the Romans came down upon them and took them utterly, then arose temples and baths and circuses, and of these ample evidence remains. Of the aqueduct which brought water from a spring ten miles off, near Pontsur-Vanne, several fragments have been found, and traces of another between Paron and Collemiers, villages on the opposite or south-west side of the city. In a field on the same side, just where the little river Vanne falls into the Yonne, are the large foundations of La Motte du Ciar, an immense Roman edifice, of which the use or former appearance is unknown; some writers suppos-

ing it to have been a pretorian camp, others a temple of Ceres. On the edge of the Vanne a few yards of the wall yet remain; the rest is a mere stony site, on which neither grass nor corn will grow, but which is profusely decorated with tiny wild-flowers, finding their nourishment in the innumerable crevices. Here and there clear water has collected in the depressions, which betray by the squareness of their outline that a bath, a chamber, or a corridor, once existed upon these foundations. I sat sheltered from the wind in a corner slightly below the level of the surrounding field, and imagined myself at Ostia, where similar traces of the footsteps of that mighty people lie imbedded in the rich plain of the Tiber, forbidding the ploughshare to traverse each spot of which they took possession three thousand years ago, at the risk of breaking shaft and share against even the last prone vestiges of the power of Imperial Rome.

Of the Roman roads which went from Sens to Alise (Alesia), to Meaux (Tatinum), to Orleans (Caenaso-Genabum), and to many other places, some traces and much exact knowledge remain to us; but the very antiquity and stability of the town has naturally involved the destruction of ancient causeways, inasmuch as being constantly used, they had to be constantly renewed from age to age, and sometimes the stones were taken up to make a new route to the right or the left of the old one. A learned engineer, M. Jollair, has carefully described two of these roads, and the geographer Pasumot has dealt with others. The Itinerary of Antonine, and the Theodosian Table, may be referred to as the most ancient authorities on this part of Roman Gaul. In the meantime the reader can imagine the fair city, with its colonnades and statues, throwing out straight rays of communication across those fertile hills which girdle the valley of the Yonne, up hill and down dale, with pertinacious linear regularity, while the legions moved along them from city to city, and the prefects journeyed in state from charge to charge. The best preserved of all is that from Sens to Orleans; it crossed the Yonne

due west, and went straight up the steep hill, behind which the sun sets in April, till it reached the high land at the top. It is now a deep ravine, hollowed out by the rain between steep banks of chalk. This ravine, overhung with trees and bordered with wild flowers, is very picturesque. It was market-day at Sens when I climbed its steep pathway, and the country-folk were taking it as a short cut to the village on the table-land of La Gatinais. It can be traced a long way, rising and falling over the monotonous undulations once covered with forest and great pools of water.

With Roman antiquities must be classed the walls, of which a few melancholy scraps remain. Alas! It is but thirty years since they were perfect in their stately strength as when first built to repulse Teutons and Franks in the fourth century. The lower portion was composed of three or five rows of immense blocks of stone, placed one on the top of another, without mortar. These had come from the ruin of huge Roman edifices, as shown by the sculpture l'ound on the inside of many, and also by the square holes evidently intended for the insertion of iron cramps. When the walls were taken down in the reign of Louis Philippe, the bas-reliefs and inscriptions, hidden amidst a mass of masonry of houses built up on the inner side, came to light, and the chief of these were placed in the town museum. They are of the same type and the same dimensions as those found at Dijon and Autun; and they may have been once cased in marble, like those of Orange, Nismes, and Aries. Fragments of marble are found lying about near La Motte du Ciar. But to return to the walls. Above these huge blocks of sculptured stone was a thick band of bricks, separated into portions by string-courses of finer and redder bricks, as may be seen any day in various parts of England. And in the Middle Ages a stone crenellatus was added to the top. This grand girdle actually repulsed the Wurtembergers in 1814. Why twenty years later it was demolished, leaving only a fragment here and there, where some college or convent happened to be firmly glued to its side or perched upon the top, must be asked of the ghosts of the mayor and town-council, and of the government of Louis Philippe.

We can hardly exaggerate or even realize the change which passed over the cities of Gaul with the introduction of Christianity,—a change which told upon the architecture like the gradual transformation of a dissolving diorama. Eoman towns had neither towers, nor spires nor domes, except such a vast but low curve as that of the Pantheon, which is indeed the only example I remember. Everything in Roman architecture arranges itself in long lines, like the architrave of a glorious colonnade. Even the amphitheatres were *level* in their design—so many level lines one above another. There was a total absence, in public and private buildings, of that spirit of aspiration which causes Gothic architecture to break upwards in fretted towers and pinnacles,—the fountain spray of an interior prayer.

It was in the year 270, while yet the beautiful *Agetinicum* reflected itself in the waters of the Yonne, and while the neighbouring hills, rich and green as today, were sprinkled with villas built after the model of Tusculum and Ostia, that the first stone of the first Christian church was laid by St. Savinien, at the furthest end of one of the richest suburbs of the town, to the east. Here the saint met with a violent death; and here his remains were carefully interred by his disciples. The church was rebuilt in the fifth century, and again in the eleventh. The crypt of Bishop Leotheric, constructed A.d. 1001, is still in existence. Four celebrated inscriptions, referring to the martyrdom, are upon its walls, and the great stone covering the altar is the very one on which St. Savinien was offering Mass when he was struck from behind. It was broken at the Revolution, but the pieces have been carefully reunited. The upper chancel has been sadly altered and pulled about; sometimes, as in 1795, with a view to devastation, at others, with the laudable but ill-secured intention of embellishment. The lower story of the bell-tower has been improved

with the rest; but the upper part preserves its steep, slate roof, and the two beautiful ogival windows on each of the four sides, which date from the first years of the thirteenth century.

Such are the remains of the first Christian church of Sens; but from the fifth century the religious establishments of the city began to increase and multiply. All through the century of Charlemagne, that of St. Louis, and onward through the Middle Ages, until far into the eighteenth century, the Metropole Senonaise presented a noble assemblage of Gothic monuments,—St. Benoit, where St. Thomas a Becket took refuge in 1164; the Benedictines; the Celestines, now the College; the Cordeliers, where the celebrated Jean Cousin had painted some of the windows, but where, alas! the hand of destruction fell with total ruin in 1794; the Jacobins, or Dominicans, of which the church is now a barn, and where Giles Charonelles, son of a poor fisherman, first became a monk; and where he died, though at the time General of his Order, and Grand Master of the Sacred College at Rome; St. Jean, an abbey church of great beauty; St. Leon; and St. Maurice, with its great gable-end and sharp little spire rising so picturesquely from the island between the two bridges and over the Yonne,—such are a few only of the buildings which once made Sens so rich in architectural delight. I must not forget St. Pierre-le-vif, founded in the middle of the sixth century by Ste. Theodechilde, a king's daughter. The vast fortified buildings of this famous abbey were almost entire at the beginning of the Revolution. They were bought by the Cardinal Lomenie de Brienne, archbishop of Sens, for a residence. Later, he proposed to make over the magnificent church to the Faubourg. Will it be eredited that the inhabitants obstinately refused the gift, alleging a perfectly futile reason? M. do Lomenie then caused the building to be rased to the ground, all but the crypt, which subsequently crumbled of itself.

In fact, such ruin has fallen on the beautiful City of Churches, that when one now stands upon the western hill,

and looks down across the broad river, one sees the picturesque but level town lying on its brink,—here and there a spire or a tower; but in strong pre-eminence, and wholly unsupported by its whilom garland of religious houses and attendant churches—the great cathedral of St. Etienne. It rises like a vast chiselled rock from the heart of the town, and we are in a hotel nestled close to its great western front: so that when we put our heads out of the window, we have to look up and up to where the yellow light is just gilding that ornate sixteenth-century pinnacle, which somebody put up quite at the top, as an after-thought, and round which the birds are always wheeling. It is a charming irregularity, which adds both to the grace and, by contrast, to the substantial grandeur of the glorious pile.

In the matter of architectural description it does not answer to be too technical; perhaps if the reader is told that Sens is the sister of Canterbury, and that some of the same architects—notably William of Sens—were employed on each, it will best paint the edifice to English eyes. St. Thomas of Canterbury took refuge in Sens, and was long a resident here during his contests with the king.

The first foundation of St. Etienne is due to St. Savinien, who is said to have dedicated a small chapel to the Virgin on the site of a Pagan temple. Like the innumerable French churches which really date from the earliest ages of missionary Christianity, that of Sens got burnt, pulled down, and rebuilt three or four times before the commencement of the noble building which has descended to us. It was St. Anastase who began to lay, in 972, the immense foundations of the present edifice. We find Philippe Augustus building at it two hundred years later; and the huge northwest tower, called the Tour de Plomb, is of his epoch. The corresponding south-west tower fell on Easter Monday, 1267, and it was not completely rebuilt in its present magnificent proportions for nearly three centuries, the Petite Tourelle at the corner being the crown and finishing.

Vast, lofty, nobly arched, with a profusion of painted glass windows, some of which are from the hand of Jean Cousin; eighteen side chapels, one of which is dedicated to St. Thomas of Canterbury, and another contains the extremely beautiful tomb of the Dauphin and Dauphine, parents of Louis XVI.,—such is the interior of the cathedral of Sens. When the early morning sunshine streams from the east through the great painted windows, casting brilliant tints upon the universal white, the impression of peaceful splendour is something wonderful. One remembers how St. Louis was wedded here in 1234, and how, five years after, he and his brother Robert, humbly clad in simple white garments, passed through the great west doors, bearing on their shoulders the *chasse* containing the Crown of Thorns, followed by a great crowd of nobles and common people, habited in the quaint and beautiful costumes of that age.

And in the Sunday afternoons of Lent, when a whiterobed Dominican is preaching the *careme,* and the great nave is covered with an attentive auditory, who occupy every inch of floor where the sound of his impassioned voice can possibly attain, St. fitienne shows another kind of grandeur—that of the living church. And when the slow Gregorian chant—which I do not love, for there is something fearful to me in those long-drawn notes—pierces the aisles, it seems as if St. Etienne lifted a warning voice of doom and judgment among the sons of men.

And when at ten o'clock at night one of the two great bells—either Savienne or Potentienne—calls solemnly over the valley of the Yonne, as if it said " Good night" to all the village churches far and near, I remember the tradition of that other famous bell, baptized Marie, which St. Loup, the Archbishop of Sens, caused to be rung during the siege of the town by the Norman and Parisians in 615, and which frightened them so that they took to flight. Marie has disappeared, as might be expected after a lapse of twelve centuries; but Savienne and Potentienne are only 307 years old—quite youthful, in fact. They

are of enormous weight, and are hung on huge wooden supports in the top of the Tour de Pierre. A few years ago it required sixteen men to ring them; but such great improvements have been wrought in the mechanism that it now takes only four.

How often have I crossed the square before the west front while one of the bells has been calling, calling, calling, from aloft; while the market people have been sitting in picturesque groups all over the pavement, their brilliant flowerstalls displaying early roses and little pink and white camellias in charming contrast with the grey fretted stone!

The great portal suffered cruelly at the Revolution: twelve statues of the Apostles were broken, and only the wrought dais or crowns remain: but the central pillar dividing the two portions of the chief door is very remarkable; it is draped with the vine, and is faced with a fine statue of St. fitienne, which did not suffer in '93, because upon the open book which the martyr holds in his venerable hands is the inscription " Livre de la Loi " Had one letter been different, and had St. fitienne chanced to have offered to those who passed his portal the Livre de la Foi, this noble statue would assuredly have shared the fate of the surrounding ones. Above the portal is a large ogival window of about the same size. It was filled in 1579 with painted glass by one Jehan Grillot; but this glass was shivered in 1638 by the firing of the cannon in front of the cathedral on the occasion of the birth of Louis XIV. One must, however, pardon the involuntary libation in honour of the heir desired for twenty childless years, and confess with regret that the real injuries to St. Etienne de Sens have been purposely committed; and that not always with any evil intent, but from a mania of improvement at a time when taste was degraded. Above this ogival window are three colossal statues, Christ bestowing benediction and an adoring angel on either side. These are quite new, and whiter than the rest of the facade, because they are the reproduction, as far as old Gothic sculpture *can* be reproduced, of figures broken

by order of the chapter about 1730, to make room for an enormous sundial, made at the expense of the then archbishop, Tristan de Sallagard.

Again, the stranger who stands in the great nave, and sees springing up around him the forest of arches which date from the best time of French art, will lament to observe the high altar surmounted by an immense gilded baldacchino supported on four Corinthian columns of marble. This was put up in 1742 by Archbishop Languet, after the design of an Italian architect, Servandoni, in the place of the old altar, with its ancient crucifix and its beautiful and curious columns wrought in copper, all of which dated from the early part of the middle ages, but which in 1742 they found *vieux et tres-mal fait.* So likewibe the great screen and two altars, at one of which (that which was to the left) St. Louis and Marguerite of Provence knelt to receive the nuptial benediction, were destroyed in 1762, by Paul d'Albert de Luynes, Cardinal Archbishop, to make room for an objectionable screen in the most pompous style of the last century. The stalls of the choir, with their great panels of carved oak, were also put up in the last century, in the place of the ancient stalls, which were considered ugly, but which we should, no doubt, now think extremely beautiful. In the centre of this choir once stood the mausoleum of the Dauphin and Dauphine, since removed to a side chapel. The life of this prince, commonly called "Le Bon Dauphin," was written by the Abbe Proyard, and is a delightful old-fashioned book, to be found in public libraries, or picked up on bookstalls. He died, in the flower of his age, at Fontainebleau, to the grievous regret of the French people. Had he lived to reign, the "Bon Dauphin" might perhaps have done something to avert the Revolution, for he appears to have had a firmer hand than his excellent son, Louis XVI.; and he was wide awake to the strides made by the philosophical party in France. But he was cut off by consumption at thirty-six, and buried, *as* he desired, in the cathedral of the diocese in which Fontainebleau is situated. His excellent young wife did not very long survive; and the two reposed together till their tomb was rifled at the time of the Revolution. Their bodies were then thrown into the public burying-ground, with all the revolting coarseness and carelessness of the time. The fosse was too small, and "Le Sieur EdmeHubert Verot, ancien religieux Dominicain," who found himself on the spot, helped to arrange the corpses in their new resting-place, by encircling the wife with one arm of her dead husband. Such was the evidence given when in 1816 the bodies were sought for and replaced in their tomb.

"Lugeat Gallia virum principein, Omnibus naturae donis ornatum,"
runs the royal epitaph put up in 1774. The whole inscription is exceedingly beautiful, but contains a painful satire on those who cared nought for the noble character of him who was emphatically—

"Fide securus, spe firmus, charitate ardens!" whose short life was full of faith and hope, and of the tender charity which is greater than these!

In the Tresor of the cathedral is preserved an immense velvet mantle, sprinkled with the fleur-de-lys, which was used in the anniversary services for the Dauphin and Dauphine. These were undoubtedly continued up to the close 01 the reign of their last surviving son, Charles X. Various otner precious objects escaped the revolutionary thieves: ivory coffers; an ivory comb, said to have belonged to St. Loup; tapestry of silk and gold, supposed to have been presented, towards the end of the fifteenth century, by the Cardinal Louis de Bourbon Vcndome, Archbishop of Sens. But English eyes will look with far greater interest on the *armoirc,* in which are kept the vestments of Thomas a Becket; chasuble, aube, stole, and mitre. This prelate when at Sens inhabited the neighbouring abbey of St. Colombe, which is a little way out of Sens on the road to Paris. It was one of the first houses founded in Gaul, and had a splendid church, with the tomb of St. Colombe supported on white pillars in the middle of the nave; and at his feet

the tomb of St. Loup. The abbey was moated, and the fosse supplied by the water of the Yonne; it suffered from the Huguenots in the sixteenth century, and from fire in 1608. Only fragments of the old building now remain, incorporated in a convent, which occupies the old site, and is still girded by the ancient ditch, and where the antiquary will find much to interest him, though little that can recall the former splendour of the place.

It remains to speak of the archeveche, and somewhat also of the singular picturesque beauty of the streets of the town. The cloister of St. fitienne, where lived the canons, was originally on the north side of the cathedral. It was burnt in 968, and when it was rebuilt, Philip Augustus allowed it to be fortified with strong walls. There were five gates to the enclosure, of which the last two were only destroyed in 1832. The well of the cloister was considered a *chef d'aeuvre* of architecture. It is still there, of course, but a mere mass of stones; and the cloister is nearly all gone, with the ex6eption of a very pretty building, dating from the *renaissance.* A. *portecochere* leads through this building into a sort of large court, under the immediate shadow of the cathedral. In this court is the well, and the studio of the only photographer of Sens. He is the son of the *Suisse;* and is a very picturesque young man, with his hair flying down his back. He looked, taken in connection with his singular dwelling, exactly like one of the heroes in Goethe's prose novels.

The archeveche once formed part of this cloister; but after the fire, Archbishop Sevin rebuilt it on the opposite or south side, and left the canons to themselves. Then first was planned that noble hall which now, in restored beauty, raises its high-tiled roof, and six enormous ogive windows, on a line with the west front of the cathedral, and which is large enough to form a conspicuous portion of the whole pile as seen from any part of the neighbourhood. Five large statues in stone are placed on the buttresses which divide the facade; in the middle is St. Etienne, and to the right

and left St. Savinien and St. Potentien, first apostles of the country. Adjoining the cathedral is Pierre de Charny, under whom the hall was restored after the fall of the Tour de Pierre in 1267 (which ruined nearly all Archbishop Sevin's work), and on the opposite side is Louis IX. (St. Louis) on his knees. Under the hall are huge vaults, lighted in the inner court by strong barred windows,—and the awful prisons of the middle ages, into the lowest of which entrance can only be obtained by descending a ladder. Tradition says the condemned prisoners were let down by ropes.

Behind the hall, and due south of the cathedral, is the archeveche. The present actual abode of the archbishop is a great pile (not deficient in a certain grandeur, though wholly wanting in sculptural detail), built in 1557 by Cardinal Louis de Bourbon. But far more beautiful are the remaining portions of a somewhat earlier date, which stand atright angles to the main dwelling, and were built by Archbishop fltienne Poncher, in 1520. His palace was rich in all the delicate ornamentation of the *renaissance;* the pilasters, cornices, and window-frames were all wrought with the finest work of the age.

In the early part of this century, fltienne Poncher's archeveche stood entire, but much dilapidated, and the damp soaked through the walls. Monseigneur de Cosnac offered three thousand francs for making the most needed repairs, such as stopping the holes in the roof. This small sum would have sufficed to keep the beautiful and venerable building for some years from further decay. The offer was refused, and demolition actually began at a cost which would have preserved the fabric to posterity. Three-quarters of the first story were pulled down, and the finely-sculptured fragments lay for years scattered over the court; after which they were heaped one on another to make room for th3 new stones required in the reparation of the cathedral. The long low building which stretches down part of the Grande Eue, yet shows how lovely the edifice must have been; and entrance to the south transept door of St. Etienne is still gained by passing into the court through a beautiful little door of Etienne Poncher's, graced with luxuriant foliage and rich arabesques. Within is a small staircase-door, also adorned with sculpture, partly Gothic, partly of the *renaissance;* to the right of which are large windows divided by stone mullions, all equally rich. To the left is an elegant well; and in the days when architecture was a familiar art, wells offered an opportunity for beautiful ornamentation which we seem to have quite forgotten in these days.

It may perhaps seem spiteful to record that it was the year 1832 which brought about the demolition of half Etienne Poncher's archeveche. Decidedly the chief functionaries must have had a spite against the arts; they made of their beautiful Sens *une mine habUe'u,* and the squares and promenades of the town were scattered over with immemorial stones and broken sculpture, It was probably because they thought it too insignificant that they spared a housewall in a street running into the Grand Rue, built by some enthusiastic inhabitant in 1547. He chiselled delicate little patterns up and down his door and window, and round shields and panels; his device appears to have been three hearts and a hammer, and he sprinkled inscriptions in Greek and Latin to the effect that the best house was the house of friends, and that he dedicated his dwelling to

"Unus Deus et plures amici."

Ah! the pleasant days when men built their houses after their own minds, and wrote their own devices on the walls, and none laughed at them; when little wooden knights and saints peeped out from the angles of the gable-ended houses, and every street displayed a store of imaginative wealth. Many beautiful nooks and corners yet abound in the city of Sens; grey walls covered with golden wallflowers, above which the Tour de Pierre is seen shooting up into the blue sky; and gardens where the wheeling pigeons whirl about with the great grey mass of the cathedral for a background; and river brinks where the poplars reflect themselves in the still flowing tide of the Vanne and the Yonne, intermingled with the spire or tower or softer image of the passing sail.

A peaceful place is the old city of Sens, in the green valley of the Yonne, and a glorious type of the Everlasting Home is its fair white cathedral; a place wherein to lay down with a thoughtful heart the burden of past mistakes and past sorrows, and to await with prayer the dawning of a new life.

LES SCEURS GRISES. rpHE sun was setting over Rome, In glory of the April skies,
And lit with smiles the convent home, Beside the church where Tasso lies.
When just below I sought the roof
    To the " French Sisters" late assigned,
    Set from the busier streets aloof,
    For tranquil heart and tranquil mind.
I bore a message o'er the sea,
From a far convent in Algiers,
    Where one remembered tenderly
Companions of her early years;
    And knowing whither I was bent
(Where that small band were newly come), By me a pious greeting sent
    To her community in Rome.
She had not seen those friends for years;
    She scarce would see their faces more, Till far beyond this vale of tears,
    The one great meeting shall restore
    The scattered labourers of the Cross,
Who part to do their Lord's behest,
    To Him who heals each earthly loss
With increase, in His Place of Rest.
    Ah! glorious will that gathering be,
From every clime, of every race,
    When hearts long lonely here shall see
Him and each other face to face.

AUX DAMES SEULES.

JDEFORE I forget them, let me write down the experiences of a two days' journey across France in the Ladies' Compartment. These long days of *petite vitesse,* especially if you are off the main lines, are apt to be exceedingly amusing; and in this instance I was going on a route seldom traversed by the English—from Bourges to Lyons; say at an angle of forty-five degrees!

Let me observe, *par parenthese,* that Bourges especially deserves a pilgrimage. The last centre of royal power ere Jeanne d'Arc restored the sceptre and the crown; the birthplace of Louis Onze, of unblest memory; the seat of an antique archbishopric and a glorious cathedral; the city in which Jacques Coeur carried on his vast commercial operations, and built his splendid house,—Bourges is splendid in its memories, rich in mediaeval architecture, almost uninjured by the reckless hammer of the *demolisscitr,* and offers a new route to the Mediterranean traveller, instead of the great hackneyed highway, which we all know by heart. After a Sunday and a Monday at Bourges, then it became necessary to move on; and it appeared that, by dint of certain changes and junctions, it was possible to strike upon the main line a little beyond Lyons. I therefore took a second-class ticket for the nine o'clock morning train, and left Bourges, with its immense cathedral standing up grey and misty against a white sky, seen through poplars and fruit trees, which were just beginning to think of the first faint green of spring.

Now it is said that on the Continent none but fools or English think of ensconcing themselves in padded first-class carriages; and certainly no nicer conveyance than the wellcushioned second-class need be desired; and there are such a large class of respectable people living on *very* small incomes (a much larger class than with us), that it is only natural that comforts should be arranged for them on an economical scale. One effect of this principle is to be seen in the cafes, hotels, and public carriages. Millionnaires are so few that there is little use in considering *them* on any large scale. Handsome fortunes belong to a few of the manufacturing towns. But the commercial genius of the country naturally exerts itself in satisfying and getting a reasonable profit out of that immense mass of moderately paid officials, small *proprietaires,* economical *cures,* and frugal shopkeepers, who make up the staple of the middle ranks of *la belle France.*

The little plump lady whom I found sitting by herself in the "*Rfyervi aux dames*" had made herself comfortable with shawls and bags, and a snug brazier for the feet; and no wonder; for she had travelled all night, coming from beyond Tours, and thence to Orleans, where she had had to wait four hours; this agreeable interval having been from two o'clock to six A.m.! The brazier had a handle by which it could be held in the lap, or applied to any part of her wellenveloped little person. She lent it to me, explaining that it contained *une brique,* which when lighted lasted several hours; a sort of combustible cake it appeared, of which you could take a supply—cold. This little lady was going to Moulins-sur-Allier, to visit her brother, who was *tin militaire.* She was mildly uncommunicative, and curiosity was useless in regard to her. Her personal appearance reminded me of a fowl which has puffed out its feathers, and allowed its head to sink luxuriously into its neck. Her brother, the *militaire,* who came to fetch her at Moulins, was at least ten years younger—*possibly* forty-five, buckled and strapped into youthfulness. She waddled off, clinging to his arm, looking incongruously affectionate; probably she had brought him up as a motherless boy. One tries to fabricate these little romances to beguile the long days of travel.

When this little lady got out, she did not leave me alone, for the junction at Saincalge had furnished one quiet Frenchwoman, going all the way to Nice to the home of her son; and at Moulins I was pleased to see a seat taken by a stout, fair Sister of Charity, clad in the thick blue gown and white-winged cap of the world-wide order of St. Vincent de Paul. The stout Sister was very accessible, and we beguiled the way by numerous questions about the rules of the order and the especial work in which she had been engaged. As the train stopped at every station, there was plenty of time for conversation. She told us that she had come from a small town in Auvergne, where forges were carried on, and that the master of one of those establishments had made arrangements with the superioress of the Sisters to have his workpeople superintended. Our travelling Sister had been fully engaged among them; she looked after the wives and children when they were sick, saw to the school attendance, and was referred to in cases of poverty or accident. So far as we understood her account, she lived with her community, but was busy out-of-doors most of the day. "Was she not very sorry to leave them?"—"Yes, very sorry; but the superioress had received a pressing letter from a house in another town, saying that they were in the greatest want of another Sister to mind a hospital, and so some other arrangements were made about the people at the forges, and she had been sent off to the vacant post. Indeed, what was one to do? If one worked for the love of God, one could not pick and choose. Not but that it was very sad to leave one's people! But, dear me, this life was short, and if one got well to the end of it, what did it matter how unpleasant it was? Perhaps, indeed, one ought to rejoice if it *were* particularly unpleasant." The Sister said all this with a sort of melancholy placidity; she was evidently quite unused to travelling, and the amiable heartiness imprinted on every line of her plump, comely face was for the moment under a faint cloud. But worse was to come. An evil spirit of curiosity prompted me to ask her in what town her new services were required.

"I am going to Nevers," said the stout Sister.

Consternation fell upon the hearts and faces of her two listeners.

"But, *ma soeur,* the train is for Lyons!"

"*Eh bum,*" replied she; "but that gentleman told me *precisement* that I must take my ticket for Lyons and go thence to Nevers." (Nevers is considerably *north* of Moulins-sur-Allier, and Lyons a long day's journey to the *south.)* "But, *ma sceur,* we are getting further and further away from Nevers every minute."

The good soul turned her fair placid face full on us, and stared with an expression of bewildered helplessness, which went to my heart. I took her hand and tried to comfort her, telling her that after all she could get a return train later in the day. But she only ejaculated, while the tears came to her eyes, *"Mais, ma bonne dame, ja me fait malade."*

Then we fell to consultation as to what was best to be done; and the sensible lady bound for Nice advised the Sister to get out at the very next station, and retrace her steps by the first train going north. But, alas! when we came to examine the Continental Bradshaw, we found that there was no northern train until so late in the day that she could not have reached Nevers before the community were gone to bed. The rational thing would have been for her to have returned some way up the line, and got a bed for the night—say at Moulins, where we had picked her up, and then have proceeded to Nevers by an early train. But no power of explanation on our part would have ensured her doing this safely. She had it firmly on her mind that she had taken her ticket for Lyons, and to Lyons she must go. "The gentleman" had told her so. What that officious individual's head was made of we of course never knew. He and his wife (for he was travelling with a wife, which circumstance had probably increased the stout Sister's profound reliance on his advice) were far away by this time from the reach of our indignation or the tears of his victim!

On reference to Bradshaw, we there discovered that once at Lyons, the stout Sister would do best to return north K by the main line to Paris, branching off to Nevers at some junction not far from that town; and on the great trunk artery of France there was less chance of her getting strayed and pounded. This settled, and a gleam of comfort reappearing on her mild face, we inquired where she would sleep at Lyons.

"I shall go, *chere dame,* to one of our houses, and ask for a bed."

"And what will you say to the superioress?" we asked, with a certain *malice. Un fin sourire* quivered upon the lips of the stout Sister, which for the moment revealed all her nationality, and quite altered the cast of her somewhat Saxon features.

"Ah! *chire bonne dame,* I shall get in quite late, you know, to Lyons, where probably the superioress will ask me no questions, and then the train starts at five in the morning, so that I shall not need to say anything of whence I came, *only that I am going to a hospital at Nevers."*

This matter settled, the Sister recovered her equanimity, and our party of three conversed pleasantly while the train rolled slowly along. To our right the snow-clad mountains of Auvergne appeared in the distance, seen through drifting showers. The afternoon was peculiarly cold for March, and the hilly country to the left, near which late in the day we wound our way, showed grey and cheerless in the waning light. We passed Roanne, a busy, thriving town, up to which the Loire is navigable, and where we began to touch upon the great manufacturing sphere of busy Lyons. From Roanne to St. Etienne, at which large town we were due at a quarter past eight, we still followed the Loire. The railroad between these towns was the first constructed in France, and horses, not locomotives, were originally used upon it. At Montrond, a village on the river, is a noble old castle, burnt at the Revolution "by order of an itinerant representative of the people." And so on, through mills and forges, nearer and nearer every moment to the great busy centres of trade, until at last we were whirled into the station at St. Etienne, "the French Birmingham," which is all coal below and coal above, galleries being even driven under some of the streets,—a great place full of ribbon factories and gunsmiths' shops. The ribbon weavers live chiefly on the outskirts, to avoid the smoke which hangs in clouds over the town; but the gunmakers hammer and test as they did in the days of the Great Napoleon, and bayonets are forged by numerous hands. At St. Etienne there was a rest of ten minutes; our French lady left us there, having friends in the town at whose house she meant to sleep. I alighted and went to the *buffet* to get a cup of coffee. I remember this trifle, for St. Etienne we were destined never to forget.

The coffee was hot, and the half-finished cup was suspended in my hand when the train-bell rang loudly. In England this would have meant "five minutes;" but not being sure of the manners and customs of French trains, I set down the cup and went hastily along the row of carriages, where porters and guards were calling and slamming doors. In the half-lighted station, on a dark evening in March, I could not find my carriage, till at the extreme end I saw a large white bonnet with white flapping wings agitating itself in an alarmed manner. It was the stout Sister, who had sat composedly while our train split into parts. In this great central station, our "ladies' carriage" had got to the hinder end, and the Sister was in a great alarm lest I should miss her and it, and all the cloaks, bags, umbrellas, etc., lawfully belonging to me. She put out a powerful arm, enveloped in the picturesque blue serge, and pulled me up the steps. I was not a moment too soon, the slamming of doors, the quivering of the carriage, and the long-drawn note of the horn by which a French railwayguard bids the driver "go on," were all simultaneously in the air, when our door was hastily and violently flung open, and a railway official, in a handsome important-looking uniform, pushed a young woman up the high steps into our carriage, where she would have tumbled on to the floor in a heap if the stout Sister had not caught her, and placed her on the opposite seat near the window, through which as we moved off, the official flung parting syllables of, "Now, Madame Bertrand, there you are—gone! You'll be at Lyons in two hours—the devil, what a race!" His exclamations were drowned in the increasing rumble; the long train cleared the vast station, and rolled out into the dusky suburb of St. Etienne, and, to our extreme consternation, the young new-comer burst into a passion of hysterical tears.

She wept and sobbed, muttering, "Oh, mon mari! mon mari!" and burying her poor little face in her hands, so that we could see nothing but the pretty frilled border of her white cap. She was very neatly and well dressed, and all her distress had not prevented her putting on that fresh cap and a handsome shawl, and taking her umbrella. She evidently belonged to that respectable class of small *bourgeoisie* whose external appointments are always so perfect in France.

It then became touching to see how the stout Sister rose to the emergency, and how her bewilderment and mild gossiping manner vanished, and became changed into a gentle motherly dignity, seeking to strengthen and console. She took the umbrella out of the trembling clutch, and with a sort of persuasive authority, extracted the pitiful little story. Monsieur Bertrand, a young man of twenty-five, had been three years married. He was guard to a luggage train 'constantly passing between St. Etienne and Lyons; he had a hard life of it; was usually up at four in the morning; and his salary was £50 a year. His wife lived at St. Etienne, kept his little home snug, and welcomed him to his occasional meals by their own fireside. On this day she had started him early, and had been expecting him home to an eight o'clock supper; when, about half-past seven, the allimportant *chef dc gare* himself,:i n an whom she never saw from year's end to year's end, had come in violent haste to her lodging, bidding her prepare to go off to Lyons by the evening express. He bore in the open telegram, " Bertrand, graveinent blessu," and told her, moreover, of the verbal account brought by a porter, that her young husband had been on his train in the long tunnel of Lyons, when a concussion took place; he had been thrown off on to the line, and something had either fallen on him or passed over him. Her mother had been sent for to him—the old woman lived at Lyons,—and now they had sent for *her.* She sobbed out that the accident had taken place at eleven in the morning, and why had they not sent for her before?

That two hours' agony is never to be forgotten. Though the train *was* the evening express, it kept stopping at station after station of that populous and influential district. Every stoppage seemed unendurable. Madame Bertrand, sitting quiet for five minutes, would suddenly burst out in an agony, saying he was dead,—had been dead when the telegram was sent. 'And though we gainsayed her vigorously, it was with doubting hearts and lips that half-betrayed their insincerity.

I had to quit the train at Givors, half an hour short of Lyons. As I left the station with a porter deputed to show me the way to the inn, the cold sleet was driving down through the darkness, and the lamplight reflected in the puddles just served to show the black and dirty neighbourhood. Yet on the morrow a cross-linc would take me on to the great highway to the blue and sunny Mediterranean; and ere four-and-twenty hours had elapsed, that cold and dreary darkness would be as a dream. Not so the human tragedy. As we left the station I asked my guide, "Was there not a bad accident in the tunnel at Lyon-Perrache this morning? Did you hear of it down the line?"

"Mais oui, Madame. Je le connaissais bien, Monsieur Bertrand. Helas! il est mort!"

And the poor young wife was even then speeding through the night, to be met at Lyons by those awful words. I was haunted by images of her arrival at the station, of the meeting with her mother, of the terrible vigil in store for her that night. Alas! for the simple household destroyed in an hour by some carelessness in dealing with the mighty monster steam. Alas! for the young man cut off in the force of his manhood. Alas! for the cruel ending of those two hours of hurrying suspense. This story rises with every detail into my memory whenever I see the ticket hanging at the door of a railway carriage, bearing the words, "For Ladies Only." MARLY-LE-ROI.

rpO these dark *grovea* a royal footstep came,
And all the woods awoke. Huge stems were felled To let in vistas of the winding Seine, While midway on the hill the walls arose Of the King's house, and round about his own Were twelve pavilions set, zodiacal Unto the king's, which was the central sun! 'Twas

Mansard built them, and Lebrun who wrought Devices for the walls, while every grove And every alley double-lined with limes, Had its own white-limbed god; and in the sun A hundred fountains played, whose waters leapt Rejoicing down the slope. A hundred years The sister arts held sway. Here Louis reigned With that strong hand of his; strong in despite Of much mistake and failure. The grave wife,

Who ruled the ruler in his older years, Kept solemn state amidst the whispering Court;
And when the pageant vanished, and the times
Changed with the men, here the gay Regent played;
And here the child, the little lovely child,
Who was the heir to France and ruined hero,
Played with his mates, Desired and Well-beloved,
Through all those early years. St. Simon paced
Those double alleys, with a prudent tongue,
And still more prudent ear; and the sweet bride,
Marie Leczinska, mother of a son
Too early lost, for whom that mother prayed—
"Take him, 0 God, and spare his father's fate,—
The shameful licence of a shameless age,"—
Mourned thro' long years of worse than widowhood.
And here the blue-eyed woman with the brow
Which never blenched before the angriest mob,
Held "mon gros Normandie " upon her knees—
Poor pretty infant! ne'er to be a man—
And pressed him to her heart.
Marly-le-Roi
Is utterly desolate now; and not a trace
Of the Pavilion of the Central Sun,
Nor of the other twelve—zodiacal—
Exists above the soil, save the hard lines
Of strong foundations bedded in the grass.
There are no fountains shining in the

light,
Nor any waters leaping down the hill.
The marble gods are gone; but still the woods
Sweep with a certain curve majestical
About the empty space, as if they held
A viewless mein'ry in their wide embrace,
And were too loth to lose it and encroach
Upon the ancient sites. On either hand
The double alleys put forth patient leaves,
Season by season, tho' no courtiers come
To plot and gossip there; the hand of man
Has ruined what he raised; but Nature, hard
To fashion at his will, retains his mark,
And witnesses with her persistent forms
The changes of his purpose.-

A DAY AT ABBEVILLE.

rjlWENTY years ago, we posted into Abbeville by night, and were deposited in an old-fashioned inn, with a large walled garden. In the morning we posted further on across country to Rouen. Since then, many a time has the Chemin de Fer du Nord borne us flying past the ancient city oft visited by English kings and English men-at-arms; not, perhaps, deigning to stop to take in water; for Abbeville, once upon the highway of nations, now lies just, as it were, a shade to one side; just a shade—the distance between the station and the ramparts. Yet this is enough to cause the *maUre d'hotel* to shake his head, and say in a melancholy accent, "Abbeville est presque detruite.'"

On asking for the Hotel de l'Europe, I was told that the Hotel Tete de Boeuf was " all the same." Which, however, was far from being the case, as neither the building nor the master was what we had known twenty years ago. *Query,* as to the degree of affinity required by the inn-keeping intellect to produce the degree of identity? In fact, the Hotel de l'Europe no longer existed. The house was possessed by a body of religious, the Sisters of St. Joseph, and their large school for young ladies. The Tete de Boeuf had been a small *chdteau;* two still picturesque brick turrets bearing witness of its ancient state.

In the morning I walked over almost the length and breadth of Abbeville, surprised to find it so large and apparently flourishing; and yet, in spite of tall chimneys on the circumference, full of the quaintest old houses in the centre. Some of them have richly carved beams running along the edge of the overhanging stories. Such may still be seen in a few English towns; I remember them at Bocking, in Essex. The glory of the place is its great church, or rather the nave, for this is all that ever got completed of the original design of the time of Louis XII., the king who married our Princess Mary, sister of Henry VIII. The choir has been patched on, and is about half the height of the nave. The latter is a glorious upshoot of traceried stone, with two towers; perhaps all the more impressive from having been thus arrested in the very act of creation. It is like a forest tree which has only attained half its development; and one feels as if it ought to go on growing, pushing out fresh buttresses and arches, till its fair proportions stood complete. There is an excellent stone staircase up one of the towers, and from the top a wide view over the town and the fields of Picardy, even to the sharp cliff marking where the sea-line must be. The windings of the Somme may be traced for many miles. I was told that the tide used to swell up almost to the town, and that several little streams, once falling into the river, were dried up. Even now, as there are several branches, one is here and there reminded of Bruges, by the little old-fashioned bridges crossing a canal in the middle of a street. A broad girdle of water seemed to me to surround great part of the town; but I could obtain no map and no guide-book, though I anxiously inquired at the best shop. Only a history of Abbeville was dug out of the museum at the Hôtel de Ville, which building has a strong and plain tower, reported of the eleventh century. The Abbevillois care little apparently for their antiquities, though they are many and curious.

This ground, though somewhat bare and barren in appearance, has been thickly occupied by humanity from the earliest ages of history. Keltic barrows have been found here in abundance, and though many of them have been destroyed in the interests of agriculture, enough remain to delight the antiquary by their flint hatchets and arrows, their urns, and their burnt bones. One such barrow, near Noyelles-sur-mer, when opened, was found to contain a large number of human heads, disposed in a sort of cone. In 1787, one was opened at Crecy, and in it were found two sarcophagi of burnt clay, in each of which was an entire skeleton. Each had been buried in its clothes, and one bore on its finger a copper ring, its dress being fastened likewise by a brooch or hook of the same metal. Endless indeed is the list of primitive instruments in flint, in copper, in iron, in bronze, found hereabouts; likewise vases full of burnt bones, not only of our own race, but of various animals —mice, water-rats,and "such small deer;" and, in the near neighbourhood, of boars, oxen, and sheep. Succeeding to these wild people and wild animals came the Romans. Before they pounced down upon us, before they crossed over to Porta Lymanis, and drew those straight lines of causeway over England, which make the Roman Itinerary look something like Bradshaw's railway map (only straighter), they settled themselves firmly in the north of France; notably, they staid so long near St. Valery (at the mouth of the river which runs through Abbeville), that they buried there their dead in great numbers, whereof the place of sepulchre is at this day yet to be seen. Their own nice neat road also had they, cutting clean through the Gaulic forests. It came from Lyons to Boulogne, passing through Amiens and Abbeville, and was in continuation of one which led from Rome into Gaul! And wherever this people of conquerors travelled, thither they carried their religious ceremonies and their domestic arts, so that we find still all sorts of medals, vases of red, grey, or black clay, little statuettes, *ex votos,* and sometimes larger groups of sculpture, such as one in bronze, representing the combat of Hercules and Antaeus. Carthaginian medals have also been turned up here, brought from the far shores of the Mediterranean; and those of Claudius, Trajan, Caracalla, and Constantine. This long catalogue is useless, save to mark the rich floods of human life which have successively visited the banks of the Somme.

In the first year of the fifth century, the barbarians made their way up to the Somme, fighting the Romans inch by inch. Attila burst upon this neighbourhood, and fixed his claws therein; the tide of Borne rolls back upon the south, and new dynasties begin, and with them comes in Christianity, not, however, without much difficulty. The faith appears to have gradually spread from Amiens, where St. Finius preached as early as 301; but even 179 years later, St. Germain, the Scotchman, was martyred, and St. Honore, the eighth bishop of Amiens, laboured daily, for thirty-six years, in conjunction with Irish missionaries, to infuse Christianity into the minds of people equally indisposed, whether by Frankish paganism or Roman culture, to accept the doctrines of the Cross. Indeed, the learned historian of this part of the country, M. Louandre, believes that even Rome itself had never been able to destroy the old Keltic religion. He says that, as late as the seventh century, the antique trees, woods, and fountains were still honoured by public adoration in this part of France; and St. Rignier hung up relics in the trees to purify them, just as in Rome itself the old pagan temples were exorcised. And after a time the old gods of all sorts were known either as idols or demons, no particular distinction being drawn among them: they lie as *debris* beneath the religious soil of this part of Picardy, just as the bones of those who adored them are confounded in one common dust.

Late in the seventh century appears St. Rignier, the great saint in these parts. He was converted and baptized by the Irish missionaries, and thereupon became a most austere Christian indeed, only, says his legend, eating twice a week —Sundays and Thursdays. King

Dagobert invited the saint to a repast, which the holy man accepted, and preached the Gospel the whole time they sat at table,—a day and a night!

We must now take a great leap to the days of Charlemagne, because in his days the Abbey of St. Rignier, near to Abbeville, was very famous indeed, both as monastery and school, and contained a noble library of 256 volumes, the greater part whereof were Christian, but certain others were pagan classics; let us, for instance, be grateful for the Eclogues of Virgil and the Rhetoric of Cicero. Of this library but one volume remains; I have seen it, and with astonishment. It is a copy of the Gospels, written in letters of gold upon purple parchment. It was given by Charlemagne to the Count-Abbot, Saint Azgilbert. This one precious fragment of the great library is in the museum of Abbeville. The school was, indeed, an ecclesiastical Eton and Oxford. The sons of kings, dukes, and counts came here to learn the "letters," of which Charlemagne made such great account.

Now, the town of Abbeville first gets historic mention in the century succeeding Charlemagne. It is called Abbatis Villa, and belonged to this great monastery of St. Rignier; wherefore I have introduced both the good saint and his foundation. It grew, as almost all the towns of the middle ages did grow, from a religious root—a tap-root, striking deep in the soil. Of course, having thus begun to grow, its history has many interesting chapters, a great deal too long to be copied or even noted here; it will not be amiss, however, to look for its points of occasional contact with England. Firstly, then, it was from St. Valery, the seaport of the Somme, that William the Conqueror set out for England. Then, in 1259, our Henry III. met St. Louis at Abbeville, and Henry did homage for his French possessions. Then, in 1272, our great King Edward I. married Eleanor, heiress of Ponthieu,— she who sucked the poison from her husband's wound; and the burgesses of Abbeville, misliking the transfer, quarrelled violently with the king's bailiff, and killed some of the underlings.

Eleanor's son, Edward II., married Isabel, the

"She-wolf of France, with unrelenting fangs,
That tear'st the bowels of thy mangled mate."
L

This unamiable specimen of her sex lived at Abbeville in 1312; but during her reign and residence, and that of her son Edward III., the inhabitants of Abbeville ceased not to kick indignantly. The King of France, her brother, struck into the contest "pour conforter la main de Madame d'Angleterre." The legal documents arising from these quarrels partially remain to us. So they go on, quarrelling and sometimes fighting, until the great day of Crecy, when our Edward III., the late king's nephew, tried to get the throne. The oft-told tale we need not tell again. In 1393, France being in worse extremities, we find Charles VI. at Abbeville, and Froissart there at the same time. Perhaps, in respect of battles and quarrels, these few notices are sufficient; I only wished to indicate that Abbeville was on the borderland between the English and the French, and came in for nn ample share of fighting. Two royal ceremonials enlivened it in the course of centuries, whereof particular mention is made in the history. Louis XII. here met and married Mary of England, in 1514,—"La Reine Blanche," as she was afterwards called, from her white widow's weeds. In the Hotel de Cluny at Paris is still shown the apartment she occupied. Louis was old and Mary young when they married; but the French historian recounts her exceeding complaisance and politeness to the king, and his great delight therein.

In 1657, young Louis XIV. came here with his mother, and lodged at the Hotel d'Oignon. Monsieur d'Oignon, the noble owner, had everything in such beautiful and ceremonious order for their reception, that he became a proverb at Abbeville,—"As complete and well arranged as M. d'Oignon." A sort of *rich* Richard.

The antiquarian who goes to Abbeville and dips into the history (by M. Louandre) at the museum, will find plenty of interesting matter about the manners and customs of the Abbevillois, rendered all the more striking by so many of the old houses being yet just where they were, and as they were. But few impressions of the book seem to have been printed off, for it is no longer sold, though the obliging librarian did say he knew where a few copies remained at a high price. This for the benefit of any long-pursed antiquary, curious in local histories. It is such a book as can only be written by a devoted son of the soil digging away on the spot.

In the Revolution, Abbeville fortunately escaped any great horrors; but the trials of the middle ages afford plenty, especially one of a certain student, condemned for sacrilege. Now, it is a peaceful, well-governed town, busy in making iron pots and cans, and other wrought articles from raw materials brought by the railway. It proves to be only in respect of the hotel interest that *Abbeville est presque detruite.* THE ROMAN CITIES ON THE RHONE.

rjlHB rain had ceased, and in the watery west
Enough of daylight lingered to beguile
A traveller's footsteps from the narrow town And past the mighty wall, beneath whose shade The streets have clustered, to the tranquil road Which leads to Orange from the distant north. And there, on my amazed and ignorant eyes, Rose the fair span of a triumphal arch,— A strange pathetic witness of the chains Which Caesar fixed on Gaul, and b6und her fast With network of his causeways, east and west. I passed beneath it, as the evening fell Misty and golden-green with southern March; And looked up at the sculptures undecayed, And at the vast proportions, square and strong, In which Rome wrought her masonry. It seemed

A strange, sad exile from that dearest land
Where stand the other three, beneath the crests
Of Capitol and Palatine, and groves
Which crown the churches on the Coelian Hill.

But Nismes I saw in sunshine, when

the light

Flooded the great steps of the Golden House,

And painted it against the tender sky,

As any time within this thousand years

And half as much again. And all the Place

By which the Golden House is girt about,

Was thronged with citizens' feet, which have not ceased

Their hurrying tread since first that house was built

In honour of a god.

With Arles the same,—

Whose accents yet retain a Roman note,

Whose dark-eyed women smile with Julia's eyes

And grave Cornelia's pride; whose people sit

Unto this hour upon their seats of stone,

Spectators of the game;

For far and wide

Within the valley of the rushing Rhone,

Beneath her stony hills, and where the vine

Mates with the olive on the sunburnt slopes,

This mighty Nation of the seven mounts

Planted her eagles; and her legions laid

Their arms together while she built in peace,

And dwelt in peace for centuries.

All the land

Is vocal with her presence; the swift streams

Are spanned by her embrace, and as the Rhone

Bursts from the snow-fed crescent of the lake

Which cradles his young streams, he sweeps his

Through famous mem'ries, second but to those

Which Tiber bears to Ostia, where the waves

Of yellow water whisper to the sea

The latest word from Rome.

TEOPLE I MET ON THE BANKS OF THE SEINE.

TF English travellers on the Continent seek exclusively for "le confortable;" if they entertain a strong objection to sanded floors, and always take first-class railway tickets, they may gain considerable knowledge of the state of painting and architecture in foreign lands, but as regards the inhabitants they will return almost as wise as they went out. In confirmation of which is the fact that no head, however rough, adorns my mental sketch-book under the date of the inn at Dieppe; for was I not recommended to a huge barrack of an hotel on the edge of the shore, capable of lodging an enormous number of guests in the season, but now (in the month of May) forlorn and empty, save of carpenters and painters, who caused such a variety of draughts that my bones ache at the recollection! Here the pretty chambermaid rejoiced in the Saxon appellative of Dolly, and as for William the waiter, it was impossible to say whether he was English, French, or Suisse, so devoid of national characteristics were his pale face and mongrel accent. From the kitchen of this cosmopolitan establishment came shrieks of laughter, caused by jokes which were uttered half in French, half in our mother-tongue. The lady who appeared to be the mistress talked French when she was settling the bill, and English when she petted her dog. French was, so to speak, the legal language of the house, yet the linen, and the plates, even the very tea-cups were marked "Morgan," and instantly, of course, suggested "Jenny Jones." The only true French creatures jotted down by me in this seaport town were the polite soldier on the castle battlements, who said that Dieppe was certainly interesting enough if one passed through it; but ah! bah! when one stayed six months in garrison, with nothing to do but to walk up and down, then the fine view did not console one; and secondly, that irresistible baby on the quay. He was only eight months old; but a Frenchman down to the tip of his little toe-nails. Such airs of conquest; such coquettish whims as that boy displayed! He sat bolt upright in the arms of an old woman who said she was not his grandmother, but his aunt, his godmother, and some other relation to boot. I became quite confused with the intricacy of her explanations; the more so as her strong Norman jMtois was half stifled in the kisses she gave the child. He had no teeth,—the fine lad; but ah! couldn't he bite!" C'est bien fort," said she, showing me the vigorous little Cupid. For his toilet was entirely conducted by strings tied round his neck; so that when he was lifted or shaken he was apt to come out of his shell like a shrimp. "Ah! le petit bonhomme! Ah! le petit cochon! II est *ben* fort! Ah! ah *I"* To all of which the baby replied by a wise wink, as much as to say, " Silly old woman I They are all alike!*"*

At Rouen, chance conducted me to a small hotel near the station; comfortable enough, with this exception, that the floors did not appear to have been washed since the house was built, inducing many reflections on the different ideas of the two nations; for the food prepared in this house was far more wholesome and more elegantly administered than would be the case in an English inn of the same class; and nothing could exceed the politeness of *Monsieur* and *Madame;* except, indeed, the indefatigable kindness of *ce bon Alexandre.* Alexandre was the waiter, the factotum; with hardly a minute in which he could call his soul his own, for the lower story was a *cafe.* He was an ugly man, with a long nose, but such a gracious expression of kindness as I have not often seen on a human face. How he remembered one's little wants and fancies! How he ran up and down unwearied! I often think there is a high place reserved in heaven for waiters at foreign *cafes,* who never lose their tempers, nor seem out of spirits; but whose whole life goes in an unvarying rou.d of small harassing duties; a daily treadmill. Alexandre appeared to be haunted by a vague impression that the floor was dirty, for he was very particular in bringing me a footstool; he was also not disinclined for a little conversation, which he administered with *le dessert.* One day I hear a little child cry, and ask what it is. "Ah! c'est le petit; c'est le petit Andre; il est malade!" What, then, is the matter, Monsieur Alexandre? "Ah! 9a! il a des douleurs!" *(Douleurs* appears the generic French term for all illness, from the stomach-ache to cholera morbus or hydrophobia.) I went downstairs to ask *Madame* what was the matter. *Madame* was a goodlooking woman about forty. She was nearly crying also with alarm and agitation; she fancied the child suffered in its throat. "Indeed " said I, "then do send for the doctor without delay." "Mais oui, mais oui! je le veux bien; mais mon mari ne le veut pas! que voulez-vous,—*ces homines!"* (uttered with a sort of *booming* indignation, and a tremendous shrug, and a look of confidential intelligence, as much as to say, " What can you expect of those insensible beasts! ") *Monsieur,* who was present, laughed at his wife's anger, but he had to send for the *docteur* for all that; for poor little Andre roared so that nobody could pacify him, especially when he was "en train de toilette," that night. *Les douleurs* subsided before my departure, and *Monsieur* and *Madame* were restored to domestic harmony; but I could not quite forget the bitterness of that look and tone; and *Monsicui-'s* head in charcoal is very black indeed.

At Mantes, where I established myself for some days, I came across a whole little world. The large old-fashioned inn, once the centre of the posting on the frequented northwest road, is still lively with the perpetual arrival of *commisvoyageurs,* each in his little *caliche.* The *caleche* stands in the great courtyard; the horse in the stable; the traveller does his business in Mantes, sleeps, and eats, and sets off again. Somehow the equipages reminded me of hooded insects. They alighted daily on the hotel like flies; and a great cry arose for *dejeuner;* and a sound like the flutter of many wings; and when they drove off they would be succeeded by a new swarm, and great was the smoking and eating thereof. The establishment was managed by *Monsieur,* a goodlooking burly man with a moustache, *Madame,* a young woman, with large blue eyes and a pale face, a *chef de cuisine* in a white apron and cap, and three *bonnes.* One of these latter was a widow, and had with her a pretty little daughter about fifteen, who wore a white cap, like a tidy little maid as she

was. To these must be added a *gardr malade,* who was indeed the wife of the *chef de cuisine,* and had been fetched to nurse an unfortunate *commis-voyageur,* who had fallen ill at the hotel, and had been in bed some weeks, while his little hooded *caleche* waited in the coachhouse. "Eh! poor man; what is the matter with him?" "Mais, Madame, il a des douleurs! oui! des douleurs terribles, partout." By dint of questioning, I arrived at the conclusion that poor No. 13 had had rheumatic fever, from which he was slowly recovering. It must be confessed that there is little scientific exactitude in the description I received. I asked if the house of business for which he travelled had not sent any one to occupy the little *caleche.* No! the invalid was a valuable man, and they preferred waiting till he was well again. Notice that his nurse spoke of him as "mon malade," and always with a touch of superiority, as if he were a huge doll whom she had to wash and dress; jointed, but inanimate. *"Now,"* said she, "he can feed himself! *Now* he can even walk—Ah! mon malade. II va bien " Of the three *bonnes,* one was a chief; *une femme de covfiance*—a neat, adroit little woman about thirty, who passed her morning in rushing about the courts with plates of food for the *commisvoyageurs.* One day, at our solitary dinner, this little woman inspected my companion affectionately from head to foot, and observed, "Madame, a-t-elle des petits enfants *?"*—" Mais non," I replied; "elle est demoiselle." — " Ah! h—h—h—said the little *bonne,* turning up her eyes to heaven; "c'est beaucoup mieux, 9a!" —" Mais cela depend," said I, laughing at the fervour of her antimatrimonial sentiments. "Indeed, yes, Madame! when from being mistress *chez soi,* one sees oneself reduced to be *femme de confiance* in an hotel, running hither and thither, never a minute to oneself—here! there! everywhere! Ah, it's much better to be *demoiselle!"*—" Are you married then *V* I asked. "Indeed, yes! my husband is *gargon-boulanger.* I have two little boys; my mother keeps them*;* ah! h—h—h—h—." (Prolonged sigh and groan.) "And

why are you not all together?" I asked. "Ah! we had a little business, all to ourselves; but my husband he drank, drank, drank up everything;—et me voila! et il est tout jeune encore; il n'a que trentequatrc ans!"—" But that is terrible," said I; "can nothing be done to stop him; has no one any influence over him; has he no religion by which he could be restrained?" She gave a look of astonishment, succeeded by a tremendous shrug, and a sarcastic "Ah! 9a! que voulez-vous*; ces Iwmmes* ont si peu de religion!" Remark, dear reader, that in a Frenchwoman's mouth the expression "ces hommes" does not mean only "that particular kind of objectionable man to whom I have the pleasure to be united - " it implies also a sweeping condemnation of the sex, and involves a delicate supposition of acquiescence on the part of the listener, as much as to say, "This fact is surely incontestable." I confess that I was startled by the repetition of nearly the same sentiment twice in one week, and wondered if it did not imply an amount of division between men and women which certainly does not exist in England. In France it is always considered that her children are everything to a mother; but, with us, we hear every day at our firesides, *"Tom, my dear, get out of your father's arm-chair*and though in domestic disputes the mother sides with the children (partly from a feeling that they are the weaker party), she would nevertheless defend her husband vehemently, against all the outer world, were he the greatest tyrant living. Still more would she be far from including him among "ces hommes," whose turpitudes are beyond all reasonable question. But since Frenchwomen are truly and sincerely devoted to their little ones, it is certainly a sad custom which takes away the infant from its mother, even on the day of its birth. At this very hotel, *Madame* brought me her little daughter, on the morning of my departure, having sent for the child on purpose, from the outskirts of the town. I asked if it could walk, being fifteen months old. No, said Madame, the little one was delicate, and so was backward; at least, not perhaps exactly delicate, *mais, enfin,* the woman with whom she had been placed at nurse in the country had not dealt well by the child, and they had been obliged to remove it, not, indeed, before much mischief had been done. So saying, *Madam e* snatched her baby to her bosom, and began hugging it fondly, as if to indemnify it for former privations. Said I, " But why don't you have your little girl here with you *V* "Ah, madame! il y a des inconvenients *"* and Madame gave a shrug, which included the whole business of the hotel; and carried the child off downstairs. I felt truly sorry to leave all these kind people. I had never seen them before, and might never see them again; but it does not take four days to penetrate below the surface of a household. People will tell you their griefs and their joys, their little speculations, their successes and reverses, with very slight invitation, or with none at all; and where news does not abound, the traveller in France may learn most things by watching the direction of the universal shrug.

Not the least curious glimpses are to be obtained in the railways, provided one travels second or third class, which *third* is, in this land of small incomes, perfectly respectable, if only "ces messieurs" would not smoke, right and left. I need say no more. What a rapturous animated scene was that in which three French ladies met together, in a secondclass carriage, near Rouen, and found themselves *vis-a-vis* to an elderly nun, whom they had known in their youth. How the Sister plunged into their family affairs, and indulged in mild jokes about their husbands and children. I could not quite make out whether or no they had been *en pension* under her care; but she certainly belonged to an educational order, for she told a long story about a little girl who cried outrageously, and refused to be pacified, at leaving her; and when one of the ladies got out at a country station, the others discussed her thoroughly with the Sister; and all agreed that, so far from being aged by matrimony, "elle etait mieux, mais vraiment, oui! mieux!"—" Because," said the good Sister, nodding her long black veil, "her uncle indulged

her so; and her husband probably does not spoil her so much!" Nothing is more common than to see nuns of different orders, in the railway carriages, bound on various missions of charity; and they have a curious air of seeming to be more at home there than other women. They carry a stout umbrella, but are free from the innumerable petticoats and packages under which the rest of the sex groan; and their cheerful busy faces look as if they quite enjoyed their business trips.

I must not forget one most extraordinary character, whom I encountered likewise in the railway carriage. Scarcely had the nun and her friends disappeared when a lady entered, who instantly made an impression on the nerves like that of a jarring wire. She was the oddest mixture I ever beheld of a Frenchwoman and an authoress. Her *toilette* was essentially French, but thrown on in an untidy manner. An Englishwoman, working for her livelihood, might have been dowdy, but could hardly have achieved the particular compromise expressed in the fit of that bonnet, which tilted back in a manner that said, "Yes, I am worn by a woman of genius, but by one not wholly indifferent to personal advantages." The shawl was new; but the wearer would have been happier in a garment of any other shape. The face was intelligent and kindly, but painfully wild—fiery eyes that might have been those of the Wandering Jew. And, quoth she, in tolerable and very fluent Saxon, "Ah! you are English! I too am English—by heart, by ideas. And I have lived;—oh! in all parts—*Ecosse,* Ireland,England, east, west, north, south. I love the English. My friends here are very angry with me. I write for the press; yes, in English! I wrote for the Great Exhibition—*much*. And I write stories too*;* but I fell ill; I worked—ah, too much! Here her really fine eyes glared dramatically and I give up. I say striking her forehead, *good-bye genius."*

I felt alarmed at the vehemence of her manner (knowing that genius is allied to other things), but it meant nothing, or, at least, only implied, "I, too, am a po-

et!" For she subsided into a discussion concerning Mr. Thackeray, Mr. Dickens, Lord Brougham, the Social Science meeting at Edinburgh, etc. I asked if she knew any English literary ladies. *Yes,* she said; and she named two well-known names; but it was twenty years since she had seen them. She had, however, corresponded recently with another English lady, whom she named. "Ah!" said she, "she is a *sweet creature. "*—" Nay," said I, "I don't think the description appropriate; the lady in question has many remarkable qualities, which are not included in my idea of a 'sweet creature'". My fellow-traveller looked sharply at me. She remembered various frank criticisms she had made on England, and began to have a dim consciousness that she might have included therein the writer of these pages (as indeed she had!). It was very curious to see her quick French perception coming to the aid of her incautious,

M professional *bavardage.* She withdrew into herself, like a snail when its horns are touched. As we parted at the great station, I said laughingly, " I shall ask the 'sweet creature the name of her French correspondent." And she answered, "lama very 'umble individual; like Uriah Heep." But I have not asked her name; I do not know it, or I should not thus describe my acquaintance of an hour. To me she is but a figure passing across a magic-lantern. Good-bye, my fellow-traveller! may you recall your genius, and entertain it kindly, with wise, cherishing, and fruitful results!

THE GARDEN OF THE PALAIS ROYAL. JN the Palais Royal by moonlight, Watching the fountains play,
Are a thousand ghostly shadows
Of those who are passed away.
Shadows of beauty and splendour,
Flitting from *salle* to *salle;*
Sweetest of all among them,
Marie Therese de Lamballe!
Yet there is not a place in Paris
Where it seems less wise to dream,
Than here, where the people gather
And flow in an endless stream;
Full of their follies and pleasures,
Full of the last new thing,
Under the close-cropped lindens,

Blossoming every spring.

But for me the Palais Royal
Is full of the dnys gone by,
And the flash of the silver fountains
Is a murmur blent with a sigh;
And the steps of the people passing
Are as if they came to me
From the far, unearthly distance
Of a bygone century!

THE STORY OF A BRETON TOW.

"Far beyond the sparkling trees
Of the castle park, one sees
The bare heaths spreading, clear as day,
Moor behind moor, far, far away,
Into the heart of Brittany.
And here and there, lock'd by the land,
Long inlets of smooth glittering sea,
And many a stretch of watery sand."

  'Tristam and IseuU,' hy Matthew
Arnold.

A TRAVELLER said, one autumn day,
"Guingamp rn'a pris le coeur;" looking
back from the rising ground over the
wide valley of the river Trieux, and the
gracious old-fashioned town, and the
towers of the church of Notre Dame.
And true it is that some centres of human habitation possess a winning aspect, while others quite as beautiful fail
to charm in like manner, or at least fail
to charm the same persons. Dinan and
Morlaix are perhaps both of them more
what is commonly called picturesque;
but Guingamp appeals to the present
writer, who would like to draw its portrait for your behalf, by the good help
of M. Sigismund Ropartz, who is a son
of the soil; nor is it for nothing that
M. Onfroy-Kermoalquin rejoices in his
extraordinary name: this learned Breton
having amassed enough literary materials concerning Guingamp to serve for a
great history, instead of for a slight poetical sketch as follows:—

There are two monuments in
Guingamp which it is impossible to
pass; first, of course, is that great Gothic
church, hewn of granite, whose singular
portal is the shrine of Notre Dame du
Halgoet, a place of pilgrimage for all
the country round; and second, is that
exquisite fountain, wrought as it would
seem after the manner of some Floren-
tine artist of the *renaissance,* which
looks so inconsistently beautiful be-

neath the gables of the market-place, the
sunlight shining upon its sparkling water, and upon the scarlet berries of the
rowan-tree which feathers against the
sky. And with Guingamp are also closely connected two people, whose names
will probably be quite unfamiliar to the
English ear, Charles de Blois and Francoise d'Amboise. Long as it is since the
earthly career of each was ended, you
cannot go ten miles in Brittany without
coming on the trace of one or both; and
in this particular town their memories
are particularly alive.

It was night when we drove from the
station of the latelyfinished railway,
which has connected this far outlying
district with the heart of France. We had
passed Lamballe in the red light of the
setting sun, and the high church-tower
seemed to blush with the stain of that
fearful day in September '93, when
Marie Therese de Savoie, dear friend
to Marie Antoinette, and widow of the
Prince de Lamballe, was cruelly murdered outside the prison of La Force.
In the fading twilight we had passed a
lonely bay opening upon the Channel,
no human beings in sight except a few
women working in the fields; and beyond St. Brieux we had traversed what
looked in the dim moonlight like great
fi«o *landes* covered with low trees and
shrubs, and which by reason of their
extent had a gloomy and romantic aspect; so that the animated streets of
Guingamp, and the light which
streamed from the open portal of the
great shrine, looked particularly warm
and cheerful, and like a welcome, as we
were deposited in the courtyard of the
Hotel de France.

Early in the morning we went
through the triangular market-place, and
passed the fountain to the cathedral,
which is well worth careful attention;
for, as a French author truly remarks,
even as literature is the expression of
a living society, so are the history and
manners of a country embodied in its
architecture; and the most ample evidence is found in every part of Brittany
of the devout faith of its mediaeval population, and their untiring energy in ex-
pressing it in stone. The associations of

art-masons,—known as *les Lamballais,*
hewed and chiselled, with a faith and
patience we may well call astounding,
blocks of *Irrsanton,* a stone hard as the
diamond. It has been observed that Brittany, in respect to architecture, is a century behind the neighbouring provinces;
but we must not forget that "ce que la
Normandie modelait dans le tuf, la
Basse-Bretagne le ciselait en granit."
Thus many generations laboured on a
single church; and thus the style is often
changed from one generation to another, for ideas were modified as years
went on, and in those days of encrgetic
conviction, art was subservient to the
dominant thought of the day.

Notre Dame de Guingamp was originally founded as the Castle Chapel, and
the most ancient part of the existing
building is not older than the thirteenth
century. We may place the date of the
construction of the actual church between the fourteenth and sixteenth centuries; and this period of two hundred
years comprises the historic epoch of
Charles de Blois, Francoise d'Amboise,
and Anne of Brittany, all of whom assisted in creating or enriching this beautiful edifice. It boasts of three towers,
the centre one being surmounted by a
spire; of these a few words should needs
be said. The tower to the north-west
would of course be to the left of the person entering the great door. It is the oldest part of all, as its time-worn walls
sufficiently show. Its great windows,
which are unfortunately blocked, are
pure ogival in design; it contains a shabby old clock, and is called *la tour
d'horloge.* The south-west tower is entirely different in style; it is called *la
tour plate,* from having a flat top, and
is *renaissance* of the sixteenth century.
That we may learn how these two styles
came to be thus united, let us inquire of
the inscription in old French which is to
be seen upon the base of this tower.

"La vigille S. Andr6, vers le Boir,
La 1 cfig cents trate et cfiq,
La grade ame piteuse a voir
Fut de cette tour qui a terre vint."

And upon the west face of the same is
the further inscription,

"Au none, dit le cinquiesme jonr l'an

m....

Cinq cents trate-sait, la premiere pierre" (the rest being lost under the roof of a building) which means to say, that on the evening before the feast of St. Andre in November, 1535, the twin tower to that on the north, ogival doubtless, fell down, crashing in its fall the west portal and part of the nave; and that fourteen months later the first stone of the present tower was laid, and built in the architectural style then in vogue. Its beauties must be seen to be appreciated; description does so little to bring architecture before an unprofessional reader: whether it be of the smooth granite walls, so smooth that the interstices of the blocks are hardly visible; or of the delicate columns, carrying nothing, but blossoming at top like flowers and flames; or of the elaborate niches, or of the tall slender windows. It must, however, be stated, that the western portal, flanked by these two towers, is extremely rich and beautiful. It encloses a double door divided by a pillar, and displays a profusion of ornaments, chiselled out of the granite, with extraordinary spirit and beauty. All this was executed in the reign of Francis I., and a certain bust, in the costume of the period, has been assigned as a portrait of the king; but a more probable conjecture is, that it represents Jehan de Brosse, Due d'fitampes, to whom Francis I. had ceded the Comte de Penthievre (including Guingamp), and that a second, which is broken, was that of his duchess.

The centre, or tour pontine, must not be forgotten. It owes its name to the octagon spire by which it is surmounted: this is also of granite. It was flanked by four pinnacles, also pointed; three only remain, the fourth fell in a storm, in December, 1755. The spire itself was struck by lightning fifty years ago; and the enormous stone, which formed the point, fell through the roof of the choir, where service was being performed, but no one was hurt.

The inside of this church shows the ogival style, and that of the renaissance, combining in a curious rivalry; the one to the north, the other to the south; the one flinging up its slender columns—

"Like bundles of lances which garlands had bound;" the other disguising its heavy Roman pillars with a profusion of beautiful carvings. (Jn the four great pillars which support the granite spire, the master mason has been pleased to group together a fantastic population of brackets, displaying a series of grimacing and sarcastic heads, kings, bishops, pages, varlets,princesses,and religious women; likewise dogs, lions, and dragons. The brackets bore a world of statues, now perished. Of the other details, of the interior buttresses, of the numerous altars, of the carved pulpit, of the windows, despoiled in '93 of their treasures of painted glass, one can only say, go and look at them! It remains to speak of what is, after all, the main feature of the church, and a very important item in the history of Guingamp; namely, the chapel from whose open grillage we saw the light streaming on the night of our arrival,—the portail, as it is now called, which forms the chapel of Notre Dame de Halgoet. This famous shrine is the yearly scene, in the flowery month of July, of the Pardon, or religious fete of Guingamp; and if we inquire the origin of this fete, we must travel back to the Middle Ages, and to La Frerie Blanche—the White Brotherhood—one of those singular confraternities, of which the Freemasons' Guilds, as they exist in England, offer the only type by which we can partially realize what they were. The Frerie Blanche displayed upon its white banner this Scriptural device, written in letters of gold—

"Fun fa-mend a vec'h ez torrer," or, "a triple cord is not easy to break." This triple cord was the emblem of the three orders in the social polity— the clergy, the nobles, and the people; and the unknown founder of the confraternity wished that its members should consider each other, not only as fellow-citizens, but as brothers. The statutes were simple, combining a measure of religious observance with a public banquet, at which the members sat side by side, without any distinction of rank. Two abbes were yearly chosen, one ecclesiastic, the other lay; and the latter was

chosen from the noblesse and the people alternately. In 1456, Due Pierre, husband of Ste. Francoise d'Amboise, was lay abbe. Such was the association from which the Pardon of Guingamp derives its origin. It meets annually at the still famous shrine of Notre Dame, to which special privileges were consequently awarded by the Holy See. The Frerie Blanche exists no longer. The triple cord has been strained and broken. Only a pilgrimage, a procession, a solemnly chanted service for the repose of the souls of the ancient dukes of Brittany and the defunct members of the confraternity, remain as relics of the ancient ceremony; and for the high public banquet is substituted a dinner given by the cure to the clergy and the officials of the cathedral. "Live embers upon which," says M. Ropartz, "the wind from heaven may yet blow, awakening them to flame."

The procession, which is swelled by devout worshippers from all parts of Brittany, takes place at nine o'clock in the evening of the Saturday before the first Sunday in July. Towards sunset the groups of pilgrims begin to assemble in the picturesque streets of the Breton town. They come from the east, the west, and the south; those from Vannes and from Cornouaille are the last to appear: the road is long, and the wooden sabots are heavy. When the dwellers by the sea of Morbihan perceive from the hills south of Guingamp the massive spire, which is visible far and wide, the women make the sign of the cross, and the men uncover their grave, sunburnt brows.

All day long the church has been full of people, tapers have been burning before the famous image of the Virgin, the bells have been ringing, the organ has been playing. In the great Place near the fountain, the tents of the fair have been thronged by eager purchasers, and the Bas-Breton buys a mirror for his wife, a rosary for his old mother, and little knives for his children. Seldom does he pay much attention to the noisy antics of the jugglers; but he listens piously to the legend chanted in monotonous minor tones by the blind beggar. In the faubourgs are erected long tables covered with awnings, where several hundred people can sit and eat at ease, partaking of little fishes, fried in the open air, and of cider drunk from casks that seem to have no bottom. And while the twilight deepens, the characteristic dances of each part of Brittany are vigorously pursued by young peasants, who forget that their legs have traversed so many leagues of Breton soil ere they reached the goal of their ambition.

But the great clock of the cathedral, which booms so solemnly over the quaint roofs, the winding river, and the green hillsides, strikes nine, and the procession is about to leave the church; and never within the memory of man has it been hindered by the weather! If it poured on the morning of that eventful Saturday, evening was sure to display her unclouded roof of stars.

Out they come! into the illuminated streets. First walk young girls clothed in white; then the pilgrims in an interminable double file, each bearing in his hand a lighted taper, some enormous, some tiny—for the rich a torch, for the poor a halfpenny candle; then come the banners, the relics, the ancient and venerated statue. Tall young men, with long hair flowing down their backs, are clothed with the white robes of the Levite, and bear the statue on their robust shoulders. In the centre of the town three immense bonfires are prepared. These are lit by the clergy; "and then," says M. Ropartz, "the scene is. a fairy one indeed." The illumined houses glow, the tapers borne by the pilgrims wave, and light up the strong manly figures of the Armorican peasants with strange effects and magnified proportions; the three bonfires throw out their sparks, the smoke clears away, and a great jet of flame rises and clings to the pole which bears aloft the device of the Virgin; the fountain, surmounted by her image, crowned with flowers, throws up to heaven its threads of water changed into diamonds. There is not a spare foot of ground on which to stand; ten thousand voices repeat the pious *Ora pro nobis;* the lights of the earth deepen the blue of the sky, up to which rise at one

moment the thousand accents of a universal prayer; the faith of the people of Brittany is shown in all its ardour, with all its poetry.

And as the hours wear on, many of the pilgrims, unable to find beds in so small a town, sit upon the steps of the portail, or in circles round the ashes of the bonfires, and sing hymns together. The cathedral is kept open for worshippers, and the warm summer night allows them to seek their rest in the open air unharmed. When dawn is about to break upon the brightening east the first Mass is said, and the pilgrims begin to disperse. The long-haired peasants, with wide round hats and full breeches to the knee; the women, with richlyembroidered spencers and caps of elaborate lace, made up in shapes that vary for every district; the quaint, curious old-world figures of the antique Armorican race, have filed away across the hills, leaving pretty Guingamp to the wonted tranquillity and small activities of a small provincial town.

The history of the fountain is simple enough, but closely connected with that of Guingamp. It was originally built of lead by Due Pierre, the unpleasant husband of Françoise d'Amboise; and about twenty years after it got out of order, and the town had to pay fifteen sous to solder some of the pipes, also "compensation" for damage done to certain properties through which the pipes passed. This was in 1465; and four years later twenty of the richest bourgeois of Guingamp subscribed each a crown in advance to defray expenses connected with the conduit. This first fountain appears to have lasted about a century and a half. In 1588, the then mayor, Pierre le Goff, repaid to the neighbouring abbot of St. Croix 100 crowns, which his predecessor, Olivier Foliard, had borrowed of this ecclesiastic for the construction of a *pompe* at the top of the *cohue,* or great market-place of the town. This second fountain was, like the first, a stone basin, with leaden ornaments; and in 1696 we find an order, "that the leaden ornaments shall be placed as they formerly had been, and that the mayor shall buy back the an-

gel of stone, now in actual possession of the widow, Rene Rocancour." Also, new cement was required, and four cocks to draw off the water from the great basin. Moreover, the mayor was conjured to get the water laid on into the market, which then stood in the Place. It is not said how the ornaments came to be out of order less than forty years from their reconstruction, nor how the widow Rocancour got the angel lawfully into her possession. After this, the fountain went on for another hundred years, when the citizens determined that it could no longer be mended up, but must be entirely rebuilt, both pipes and monument. The new works were begun in 1735. The water was brought from half-way down the neighbouring hill of Montbareil by an aqueduct of more than a thousand metres in length; and a bargain was made with a celebrated Breton sculptor, Corlay, on the 28th of December, 1743, that he should furnish them an ornamental fountain for the very moderate sum of 1500 livres.

And Corlay did his work well, and in a manner that forcibly appeals to the imagination. Wholly uninfluenced by the abominable taste of the age of Louis Quinze, which seems to have spared this fair province, the vigorous intellect of the Bas-Breton artist seems to have been dominated by some dream of Italy, to which he has adapted the strength of Armorican proportions in his figures. Standing by his fountain, with its large granite bowl, encircled by an elegant railing of wrought iron, its second bowl supported by four sea-horses, the third by four sirens, and the whole crowned by a figure of the Virgin standing upon the crescent (around whom twenty slender jets of water cast their sparkling veil), the traveller involuntarily closes his eyes to shut out the stern granite towers, the gable-ended houses with massive beams and overhanging stories, and all the Gothic beauty of the North, while a far different scene looms softly out from the depth of memory; a noble mountain, girded by the olive and the vine; a fair city, crowned with walls and towers and roses and cypress spires; an exquisite cathedral of variegated marble, enriched with intricate

N design; and in the centre of an open space, beneath its shining walls, a fair fountain, of many panels, wrought in sacred device; and he mutters below his breath the sweet, soft word—*Perugia!*

The historian of Guingamp, alluding to the curious mixture of the sacred and profane in Corlay's design, remarks that, "*a tout prendre,* it was not a bad idea to place the idols of paganism beneath the feet of the mother of Him who destroyed idolatry and paganismbut that he, nevertheless, believes the sculptor did but select the " aquatic personages" who best suited him, and placed the Virgin at the top from simple piety. It was, however, the company of marine monsters which saved the fountain from the Vandals of the devolution. It was "tacitly agreed" that the statue should be considered as representing Reason and Liberty, and the fountain was respected in consequence. If Corlay had encircled the Virgin with prophets and angels, they would all have been patriotically melted down to make bullets.

But although the cathedral and the fountain are almost the only perfect monuments of the past remaining to Guingamp, mention must not be omitted of the former castle and the ramparts; and with them must be joined a few words upon the numerous sieges which the town has sustained. The *chdteau* was built by Due Pierre, and hither after the wedding feasts he brought his beautiful bride, Franchise. It was close to Notre Dame, which was originally the castle chapel; and here the young couple lived in great peace for some space of time. The Due hunted daily with his gentlemen over the wooded country, rich in game; and the Duchesse and her ladies devoted themselves to works of charity and religion until evening, when *la bienhcureuse chatelaine,* seeing her husband returning from the chase, went forth to meet him, radiant with the beauty of her youth; so that their historian declares their life to have been a little terrestrial paradise, until "the enemy of the human race" employed the serpent tongues of certain flatterers to sow dire suspicions

in the mind of the Due, and without rhyme or reason he became desperately, insanely jealous, which jealousy caused him to behave in a most moody and capricious manner to all about him, and to be unable to look at his fair young wife without gnashing of teeth; but, nevertheless, he could not exist an hour out of her presence. And one day, while she was sitting with her maidens playing and singing, Due Pierre rushed in scolding and storming, and though she cast herself humbly on her knees before him, he drove her into an inner chamber, where he beat her cruelly with freshly-gathered twigs; after which he dismissed all her servants, notably her old nurse, "a virtuous and spiritual woman," in whom the poor Duchesse placed peculiar confidence; and this last privation so sensibly afflicted his victim that she fell ill, and in a few days was at the point of death.

Thereupon the "whole of Brittany," hearing of these aborr.inable things done to a woman who was universally respected and admired, conceived great anger, and the barons addressed energetic reproaches to the madman, which apparently brought him to his senses; for he came to his wife's bedside with tears in his eyes, and threw himself on his knees, bareheaded, and asking pardon. Thereupon Francoise, like wives in all generations, forgave him without delay, and embraced him, saying, "*Monseigneur mon ami,* weep not, for I well know that this malice came not from you, but from the enemy of nature, who is envious of our good estateand so on.

All this occurred in the Castle of Guingamp, in the year of grace 1447, and the noble pair afterwards dwelt in constant amity, and Due Pierre became almost as devout as his saintly wife. When the death of his elder brother eventually called Pierre to the dukedom of Brittany, Guingamp lost its dear chatelaine; and though his will assigned the town and *cumite* to her as her dowry after his death, Francoise preferred to retire to the cloister, and the "little castle," the scene of her happiness and her trials, knew her no more. I regret to have to add that the building was taken

down in 1626, by order of the king (Louis XIII.), in pursuance of the policy of weakening the power of the nobles and the provincial towns. It is sad to read of the pickaxes and pincers, and other tools, required for demolishing the building endeared by associations of the Duchesse. It was of ogival style, like the earlier parts of Notre Dame; a portion of the towers still remains, built into the convent of the Filles de la Sagesse, who thus possess the last local relic of Ste. Francoise d'Amboise.

As for the walls of the town, they were perfect until the reign of Louis Philippe, who permitted them to be taken down—why or wherefore it is not easy to see, for Guingamp is not a place full of progress, and eager to overleap its boundaries. A few picturesque fragments of rampart yet remain here and there to tempt the artist's pencil.

Having thus spoken of the monumental aspect of Guingamp, and of the historic memories or religious associations of particular buildings, something should be said of its vital story. Until the Revolution many religious orders had institutions within its walls or in the faubourgs; perhaps the most famous was the Abbaye de Sainte-Croix, built by Etienne de Penthievre and Havoise his wife, daughter and heiress of the last Count of Guingamp. Their little boy, Henri, carried the foundation-stone upon his shoulders. This abbey played an important part in the district for five hundred years, from the twelfth to the seventeenth century, when it gradually decayed. In the Bourg de Sainte-Croix still exist several houses three hundred years old; it is now a very poor quarter. The patriots of '93, disliking the name, called it the Quartier Prairial; but it has reverted to its former appellation. There was the convent also occupied by the Dominican Fathers; their house was finished in 1234; their sermons were much admired, but they and the town quarrelled *a propos* of a tax claimed by the Fathers to aid in rebuilding their establishment, destroyed during one of the wars. The Capuchins and the Carmelites had also foundations; of thjse latter, record remains of a dispute concerning the pavement in front of their walls. The town said the nuns ought to keep it mended, and the nuns wrote off to high quarters in Paris. Down came a letter from a Carmelite Sister of great influence in Paris—no less a person than Soeur Louise de la Misericorde, who, in the world, had been Louise de la Valliere. She wrote politely, but firmly, to tell the town that she should supplicate Madame la Princesse de Conty if any more were said about the pavement; and Guiugamp submitted. The Carmelites remained there until the Revolution, when their convent was turned into a prison, into which the royalists were huddled *pele-mele.* No blood, however, was shed here.

By far the most famous, however, of all the religious establishments was that of the Cordeliers. They settled in Guingamp in 1283, and were greatly enriched by the Penthievre of that date, whose only daughter, Jeanne la Boiteuse, married Charles de Blois, Duke of Brittany, of whom it is fitting to say-a few words in this place. We select from his life of combats the English episode. In 1313, our Edward III., conceiving that his honour demanded a personal descent into Brittany, swore, says the chronicler, "to serve that felon country such a turn that it should not be forgotten in forty years' time." So he disembarked at Brest with many vessels and many men, divided his army into three portions, besieging simultaneously Vannes, Rennes, and Nantes, and himself retaining nine hundred soldiers. Four thousand archers went foraging and destroying the country as far as Guingamp, where Messire Pierre Porte-Boeuf was captain of the Bretons. Guingamp was then only defended by palisades, and the English king soon crossed the pretty river Trieux, poured his men into the town, took Messire Pierre prisoner, and pillaged the townsfolk, who were rich from naval traffic; but, as the place was not suitable for defence, Edward then fell back upon Vannes. The struggle still continuing in various parts of Brittany, we find Charles de Blois fighting four years later at La Roche-Derrien, where, on the

18th of June, 1347, (Waterloo Day, five hundred years later!) he was captured, badly wounded, and taken off to London; on which his wife, Jeanne la Boiteuse, heiress of the Penthievres, entered into negotiations for his deliverance, and the idea of a family alliance with England was even entertained, for the discussion of which interesting subject a sort of supreme council met at Dinan, composed of prelates, barons, and deputies from the loyal towns; after which six ambassadors, chosen from the three orders of the state, were sent to treat with the King of England for the ransom of Charles de Blois.

An episode then occurs in the history of Guingamp which connects it with the famous Duguesclin, who was literally locked up within the gates till he consented to lead the inhabitants against two castles held by an English captain, named Roger David, who had been wedded by King Edward to a rich and noble heiress, the widowed Vicomtesse de Rohan. Roger David worried and harried the Guingampians like the traditional ogre of a fairy tale; and when Duguesclin at last compelled him to render up his sword (the Englishman was standing behind a wagon, fighting almost singlehanded against the torrent of invaders who had burst into his castle and overthrown his guards), it was with difficulty that the French hero could save his prisoner from the angry mob of soldiers.

Returning to Charles de Blois, we find him at Guingamp in the beginning of autumn, 1364, assembling the troops of his wife's domain, and from Guingamp he went forth to meet his death. On Sunday, the 29th of September, he was struck down by the dagger of an English soldier at Auray; a few days later his corpse was brought back to the convent of the Cordeliers, in the loved little town upon the Trieux. After the custom of his times, Charles had arranged for this beforehand, and had written thus to the monks:—" Charles, Due de Brittany, Vicomte de Limoges, and Jeanne, Duchesse and Vicomtesse of the aforesaid places, to our well-beloved the Guardian and Convent of

the Freres Mineurs of Guingamp for the time being and the times to come—salutation. For that we, the said Due and Duchesse, by common assent, have ordered and chosen our burial, when God shall be pleased to command our death, in your church of the aforesaid convent of Guingamp, between the high altar and the feet of Monseigneur and Madame de Penthiiivre—whom God assist—we command and forbid, pray and require, on pain of our displeasure, that you enter no corpse, whomever or of what estate it may be, in the choir of the said church, only excepting the bodies of the founders thereof when occasion may present."

From the time of Charles de Blois' burial, the convent received the name of La Terre Sainte; and miracles were said to occur at his tomb. A legend recounts that the English soldier who killed him, having boasted thereof, lost reason and raged, on which his relations, having tied and gagged Lim, brought him to the tomb of the Blessed Charles at Guingamp, where he regained possession of his reason, made his devout orisons, gave up all his worldly goods, and entered the Terre Sainte as a monk. Twenty-one years later the widowed Duchesse, Jeanne de Penthievre, was laid by the side of her husband, and at the feet of her father and mother.

The Cordeliers received after death various other noble members of the same race; and flourished until 1591, when the building was burnt in one of the many sieges, and the monks moved half a league out of the town, on to land owned by the De Kerisac.

In looking through the annals of Guingamp for such incidents as may bring the place with vividness before the English reader, we find many signs of the commercial and municipal activity of the Middle Ages. There seems to have been a considerable foreign trade, though the town is several miles from the sea; and we find the monks of the Cordeliers in the sixteenth century putting out their money "*a fort bons interSts,*" with a merchant, which " was lucky for them," as their monastery was burnt not long after. We hear also of a dinner given to the commissioners who were organizing troops to act against Louis Ouze, and of messengers sent out express on horseback to reconnoitre the French fleet said to be in the neighbourhood; on two occasions five sous were paid to the messenger. In 1484 the seneschal gave a great supper, costing " dix sous huit deniers." Guingamp was one of the twenty-three good towns which sent deputies to the estates of Brittany: it generally sent the mayor and another; but the town had only one voice. Sometimes these deputies were paid four livres a day: sometimes 100 livres down. The mayor or syndic was elected yearly by majority of votes; the election took place on Ash Wednesday, and on the same day the community also chose the governor of Notre Dame and those of the hospitals.

It is melancholy to come across traces of the gradual way in which the royal power devoured the local liberties. The dukedom was formally united to the kingdom of France by the marriage of the Duchess Anne to Charles VII.; but it was only little by little that the system of internal government changed, and this through the finance. The royal tresor made claim to taxes which the community resisted— "Mais qui ne sait que le fisc a toujours raison V

In this town, 200 years from the marriage of Duchess Anne, in 1692, we find Louis XIV. nominating the mayor; and the *bourgeoisie,* who had in times past treated with sovereign dukes, found themselves forbidden to elect their own chief magistrate. The seventeenth and eighteenth centuries gradually reduced the Breton cities to mere provincial towns, governed from Paris. De Tocqueville has made us comprehend how, long before the Revolution, a shortsighted centralizing policy had destroyed the old local activities, and eaten into the substance of the old organization of France, leaving as it were the outward shell only, which fell before the angry passions of the mob. Had it been otherwise, had much of the old spirit subsisted in the provinces, the towns could never been tyrannized over by gangs of wretches sent down from

the metropolis in 1793. Rheims was deluged in blood,and the atrocities committed at Nantes are a bye-word; and these things were ordered by men who came down from Paris, and sent up their exulting reports to headquarters, and who were enabled to work their evil will because the wholesome local life of each province had been bound and gagged for a hundred years past. "C'etait une suite de cette centralisation fatale qui mettait et met encore la France toute entiere a la mercie d'une bande de sacripants," observes the historian of Guingamp. *Here,* however, no blood was shed; the fury of the Revolution was concentrated in Lower Brittany. But the convent of the Carmelites was converted into a prison, where 200 captives were huddled together, and made to suffer humiliation and hunger. On the 5th of March, 1794, twenty-six priests were singled out for deportation to Guiana, and a week later they were marched away, escorted by a numerous body of gendarmes, to the seaport of St. Brieux. As for the material destruction, it was here as elsewhere; the churches were shut up, turned into warehouses, allowed to fall into ruin, and finally taken down. One, that of Saint-Sauveur, was used for lodging galley-slaves; and when, in the winter of 1806, the roof became dilapidated, the materials of the building were employed to mend up another chapel in the environs. The site of Saint-Sauveur, in the centre of the town, was thus left bare; and M. Sigismund Ropartz pleads for the rebuilding, advising the War Office to part gracefully with the rich facade of the Chapel of St. Joseph, now used as a barrack store, and which might be removed without difficulty to adorn the new church.

And now for a few last words about Guingamp as it exists; for it *does* exist, and the people there are all alive at this minute, eating, drinking, sleeping, and, alas, pulling down old houses! I fear much that when next we go, that oldpeaked dwelling, standing cornerways to the marketplace, will be replaced by flat stone walls, square windows above, and shops underneath. Nevertheless the town is truly beautiful, rising as it does

above the winding river Trieux. Seen from the luxuriant garden of the Hotel de France, which is an island reached by a modern foot bridge, the cathedral forms the apex of a triangular composition; and the delicate architectural lines descend into the gables of the clustered houses, and are reflected in the water as much as a watermill and a weir will allow, while the deep shadow of the washing-sheds throws into the relief the white caps of the busy women, and the brilliant scarlet spray of Virginian creeper which trails from the roof of a summer-house across the view which I am trying to jot down on paper. As the river winds about the town, it is crossed by bridges, which afford the most charming "points," and there are plenty of poplars which stand up like spires. We walked for some distance round two sides of the town, beginning with the cemetery, a square enclosure on the east, where we wrote down some of the quaint Breton names, and gazed with astonishment at the building in one corner, dedicated to the preservation of skulls in funereal-looking boxes. It seems that when graves are not purchased *en perpetuite,* it is a common custom, after some years have elapsed, to place the skulls of the occupants in these *chdsses,* with a hole in front, out of which the ghastly remnant seems to gaze. Sometimes two skulls, those of husband and wife, or brother and sister, are placed side by side.

From hence we made our way to the hill overlooking Guingamp from the north, from whose rough side, bristling with gorse and fir, and hollowed out by a great quarry, we obtained a fine view over the ancient city with its tripletowered church. Descending again, we came upon a fragment of the ramparts, (which, within the memory of the living generation, girdled the entire town,) and followed the line to the eastern faubourg, where many of the low stone houses have an air of extreme antiquity. Pursuing the broad road for about a mile, we found ourselves constantly parallel with the Trieux, from which only a meadow divided us; and we crossed the stream by a private wooden bridge belonging to a mill, and so got into the deep moist grass on the other side, where stood a man angling for eels, a model of Breton patience, curt of speech. As we returned to the town through the meadows, we skirted a hill on our right, covered with a thick wood, which enclosed a gentleman's chateau. Several high stiles had to be crossed before we got round to the southern suburb, and so across a stone bridge back into the town. Passing the door of a decent cottage, we were attracted by the sight of two rooms, where a man and woman were plying the shuttle. The good wife entered courteously into conversation. She showed us the stuff which she sold to the peasants for aprons and petticoats at twenty-two sous the metre; and a more costly blue material, woven of wool and cotton, valued at four francs for the same length. She dealt directly with the peasants, and not with any middle-man or factory. A great air of comfort pervaded this cottage. It is true that the floor was only of hard-trodden mud; but the shelves showed plenty of crockery, and several photographs were hanging upon the walls: among them the inevitable "mon fils—un militaire." In a corner stood the great handsome bed of curious construction; the sleeping-place being perched up so high that we thought the pair would be suffocated, until we peeped under the cornice and saw there was no roof. The broad step of ascent formed the lid of a large coffer. These people spoke French; but in another house which we entered to avoid a passing shower, we found a woman sifting flour, who could not understand a word, and called out in an unknown tongue, whereat a wonderful and wizened old couple came crawling down the stairs, both of whom spoke the language of civilization.

So now here is the portrait of Guingamp, sketched perhaps with the hand of a hasty limner; but given as it appeared to one who, though but a passing traveller, viewed it with eyes that love to note every trace of the ancient civilization of France. The biography of a town is as the biography of

a man; one of the stones from which history is built. Over the beautiful site of Guingamp passed all the great traditions of medieval life. Here the church clothed herself in the fair vesture of Gothic art, and here the glorious spirit of provincial freedom had for centuries free play amidst the turbulent politics and red-handed conflicts of warlike epochs. Pious dukes and saintly women left their impression on its institutions, and give romantic interest to ita archives. Whatever is grand or beautiful in the history of France is found here in miniature; and the iron way which has so lately linked it to the centre of the kingdom, is only an emblem of the spiritual connection by virtue of which the story of Guingamp typifies the larger chronicle, whose next page is a mystery too profound for the wisest politician to decipher with prophetic eyes.

THE ROYAL WOODS. JY window looks towards the West,
Across a hill whose purple breast
Is shot with gold and brown.
And, day succeeding day, I see
The sun behind a different tree,
With tranquil beauty, bright and clear,
In this still autumn of the year
Sink softly, slowly down.
But oh! the wealth of April flowers

Which lit with joy these sylvan bowers When first we came in spring I I seem to see the bluebells lie Along the glade, as if the sky Fell lightly down across the turf, And left a bloom upon the earth.

The wind flower trembles on its stalk,
With whispering heads the lilies talk,
The primrose clings about the root
Of each grey trunk, the grasses shoot
In vigorous gladness, and the may
Puts forth its spikes of snowy spray,
Where sits a bird to sing.

Great forces of the natural heart,
Ye keep your life a thing apart,
Though kings may come and go;
The Master, whose ye are by right,
Will ne'er behold this glorious sight,
Although his Fathers, day by day,
Here held the antlered stag at bay,
And still we call our loveliest view
The royal Louis' Rendezvous.
Yet none the less this forest land,

For centuries held beneath his hand,
Puts forth its strength, renews its grace,
And clothes each wood-nymph of the place,
Though royal Louis be not here,
In varying vestures of the year.
And though the race which rules to-day
Like autumn leaves were swept away,
And all were changed as thrice before,
Yet every spring-time would restore
The beauty of the open glade,
The tender greenness of the shade;
Aud every autumn break in flame,
And bring the dyes of man to shame,
In this great after-glow,
Which lights the gold and purple breast
Of that great hill which slopes to West!

M. Maitre And His Workshops.

"JF you stop at Dijon, be sure and see the *ateliers* of Monsieur Maitre; *c'est tout* ce *qu'il y a de mieux organise'* " was an injunction forcibly delivered to a traveller parting for France. For which reason, among others, I slighted, in March, 1861, from the express train which whirls twice in every four-and-twenty hours past the ancient capital of Burgundy.

One who enters the gates of Dijon seems to pass through the magic portal of the Middle Ages. Never, surely, did any old town continue to turn up so many pointed roofs in contemptuous objection to the things that be! It is not a house, or even a street here and there nestling within its venerable precincts, but the whole town in which the people of to-day are living and working, which bears the *cachet* of the past. It did not even become an integral part of the kingdom of France until the reign of the sly King Louis XI., who got it from the Princess Marie, daughter of Charles the Bold of Burgundy, by a process which appears to have been evenly compounded of begging, borrowing, and stealing. That was the Duke Charles who plays so important a part in 'Quentin Durward,' to which novel, and to the drama so ably sustained by Mr. Charles Kean, I refer my readers who may wish to refresh their memories on the amiable monarch who possessed himself of this good town.

Dijon, clustered thickly round its

churches and convents, with the Cathedral of St. Benigne standing out in the foreground to welcome the traveller, appears to disdain any architecture more modern than that of the time of Louis XIV. The principal street is the Hue Conde; the churches date from the eleventh century; St. Benigne is said to have preached the gospel and suffered martyrdom in the year of our Lord 178. My readers will perceive that there is nothing of the "spirit of the age" in the appearance of the place, yet here is located one of the most remarkable establishments of manufacturing France, which possesses a double interest, as showing on a comparatively small and singularly distinct scale, the progress of that idea of organization which is invading (for good or for evil?) every department of human industry. I ask the question "for good or for evil," because in this point of industrial organization are involved consequences of the most momentous importance to our race, far exceeding the sphere of a single master, a single town, or even a single branch of manufacture.

Passing through the ancient town of Dijon, from the railway station on one side, to the moat and ramparts beyond the *Porte Neuve* on the other, the pedestrian (for there are no *fiacres* in the streets, even during the rainiest weather) finds himself before a large new building, standing back in a vast court. It is not very high, and is lighted by large handsome windows, and over the door, in gilt letters, is inscribed "Ateliers d'Antoine Maitre." A large shining new clock, with a face so clean that it looks as if newly washed with soap and water, strikes the hours with a clear metallic ring, which assures the ears that it, at least, never loses a minute...

I arrived at half-past three, at which hour all the workpeople are absent at dinner, and I had to wait in the porter's lodge for half an hour, whence I watched the workpeople slowly assembling: boys in blue blouses, talking and playing in groups; women in neat white caps with plaited frills, coming in twos and threes; and men very respectably clothed, some in coats, some in blouses.

Presently a little carriage drove into the court, wherein sat a stout, goodtempered gentleman, and a much younger lady, with just the same type of face, broad, intelligent, and smiling. These were the master, Monsieur Antoine Maitre, and his married daughter, Madame Leclcrc. Her husband and her little boy were also of the party. I presented my letter, and was cordially welcomed, and shown over the whole establishment, benefiting, likewise, by a very long conversation with Madame Leclerc on the state of the working classes; than whom no woman is more competent to give an opinion, so far as relates to France.

Monsieur Antoine Maitre is a master binder; a maker of portfolios, *porte-monnaics*, pocket-books, writing-cases, and albums, and the proprietor of large editions of standard religious works, such as the prayer-books used by hundreds of thousands in France, which he binds in various leathers, and with the most beautiful and elegant designs. He supplies Paris and the provinces, and even sends largely to London. His works have been created entirely by himself; he has developed the art of binding into a manufacture, according to what he himself terms "le progres de l'industrie," and he has accomplished his purpose with consummate success.

Monsieur Maitre began life as a journeyman binder, working in a small way for a master employing a few hands, as is customary in this trade. He married early, and presently obtained a workshop of his own. Madame Maitre was also engaged in the business, and worked regularly with her husband. He took in "jobs" of all kinds; re-binding a lady's prayer-book, making purses, mending writingcases, and was in all respects one of the working classes.

The work of his hands prospered, and he thought it would be a good idea to buy up an edition of some standard religious book, such as are in universal use; whether the ordinary prayer-book, a ' Paroissien/ or a collection of prayers, hymns, or meditations. This edition he would bind according to his own taste, and sell as his own. He did so, and his

experiments answered; he then bought another and another, until at length he had a printer whose establishment was wholly taken up in working for him. At the same time his trade in articles made of ornamental leather increased; and Monsieur Maitre went on adding to the number of his workpeople, and hiring additional workshops. After nearly thirty years of labour he found himself proprietor of an *ateKer* which sent its goods to all parts of France, which employed two hundred workpeople, and was very uncomfortably lodged in eight different buildings belonging to different owners, near the railway station of Dijou. The workshops were located upstairs and down, in such an irregular manner as to render the due organization of the work a very difficult matter, and M. Antoine Maitre, being what the business world calls "very comfortable," determined to build.

He fixed on a site outside the city walls, quite on the other side of the town—the side on which the Swiss attacked Di jon in the dreadful siege of 1513,—and there he erected the peaceful building which stretches its broad front parallel with the road, and bears the date of 1858. Here he employs 300 workpeople, of whom 100 are women; here he spends all his time from morning till night, "doing the work of two men;" and here he meant to build himself a large new dwelling-house, of which the foundations were already dug at the time of my visit. The air of unsurpassed neatness visible in every corner of the *atelier* is only matched by his own Dutch propriety of costume; his burly person clothed in dark chocolate-coloured cloth, his massive head and grey hair surmounted by a black velvet cap. M. Maitre is in his person and in his character a sort of cross between the modern manufacturer and the ancient burgomaster.

It is difficult to describe any industry, in writing, without being intolerably dull. I know that it used to be impossible to persuade children twenty years ago to read a certain 'Book of Trades/ even though it was amply illustrated by prints, in which industrious apprentices were working as if their lives depended on the angle of their elbows. I must, however, say a few words on the mechanical processes of this *atelier,* as the distribution and the wages of the workpeople are involved therein.

Of course the establishment is based on the opinion entertained by the proverbial shoemaker, namely, that there is nothing like leather. Vast quantities must yearly be stored in the great crypts beneath the workshops. I saw the smooth sheepskin, the rough and more expensive *peati de chagrin* token from the goat; and the scented hide of the Russian cow. All these are brought ready dyed to Monsieur Maitre, and are of every hue—green, brown, marone, and the brightest scarlet. The basement story also contains huge stacks of paper for the insides of pocket-books, sketch-books, etc., and also the printed sheets of editions of books ready for the binder's hand. These several stacks are wrapped in paper covers of different hues, so that the eye may in a moment distinguish which is which. In this part of the building are also six great furnaces, by means of which the different stories are thoroughly supplied with warm air.

The first process is that of cutting out the leather into the required shapes. The material is so expensive as to render it of the utmost importance that there should be absolutely no waste. One of the most important workpeople in the establishment is a woman, who is a remarkably clever cutter, and who is the only woman who earns as much as the men, namely, three francs a day. Each shape when cut out is neatly pared round the inside edge, so as to enable it to be turned down with ease; hemmed, as it were, upon the frame of wood or paper which constitutes the case of an article. We will take for example an ornamental prayerbook with gilt edges, such as Monsieur Maitre sends out by the thousand, and follow its stages. First, the leather is cut to the required shape; then it is stamped with a design by means of pressure between plates of hot metal, which turns out the neatest and most beautiful forms. The lines of

this design are then usually traced in varnish. This operation is performed by young girls with a delicate camelhair brush, and is very clean and easy work. It is then stitched to the printed sheets of the book, and lined with paper or with silk. The printed sheets have previously been cut perfectly even by machinery, and a thin flake of gold laid on their edges. I saw a woman laying on the gold with the utmost dexterity; but wonderful to relate, these gilt edges are afterwards polished by hand-rubbing with agate, a process which requires the whole strength of a man. If gilding is put on the cover, it is fixed with instantaneous rapidity by means of a stamp; a flake having previously been laid over the required spot. The shreds of gold which are brushed off in the process are carefully collected, sent to be melted into ingots, and then again to be rolled into flakes. All these various operations are performed by men and women sitting at spacious counters, with a distance of some feet between each, so as to allow ample room for delicate work, requiring steadiness of eye and hand. The division of labour is completely carried out, and each person only executes one process. Nothing is thus allowed for individual taste; and the "art" of binding has become a "manufacture."

The articles when completed are all brought to one spot. and separately inspected by M. Maitre. The slightest spot or imperfection causes them to be thrown on one side and sold as damaged goods. From the workshops they are carried into a vast magazine, and ranged on wide shelves. Seeing in some places a heap of different-sized articles with a list attached to each heap, I asked the meaning, and found that they represented orders sent to the manufactory by different commercial houses. When the list is completely filled up according to order, the heap is removed to a separate room to be packed in a wooden case, and thence slides down an inclined plane to the basement story, where a cart awaits it in the yard. Just at that moment, and for some months past, the great demand had been for albums in

which to insert the portrait *cartes de visite* so much in fashion; and M. Maitre could not keep pace with the orders he received. All the shreds of paper used in packing, or left when cutting out the perforated leaves of these albums, are saved up and collected together in sacks and sent to the paper maker to be remade in sheets. Of the stacks upon stacks of religious books, Madame Leclerc remarked, smiling, that if the people of Dijon became infected with *mauvaises idees* it certainly would not be the fault of her father's establishment. Many of these are illustrated with beautiful little engravings, and are quite *articles de luxe.*

The *ateliers* are large, lofty, well lighted, and thoroughly warmed with hot air. In one compartment only did I perceive anything like closeness; it was one in which several men were working together, polishing the gilding, and was a sort of glass cage enclosed in the *atelier.* In each salle there is a large basin with a cock, which turns on the excellent water of Dijon, and a metal goblet for drinking. Most of the workpeople are seated on convenient stools. The men and women work in the same salle, but there is a foreman in each, and perfect order and silence are preserved. The distance of the seats is, moreover, quite sufficient to discourage gossiping. The dress of both men and women is extremely neat. *All* the latter, young and old, wear white caps; many of them are pretty, and they have universally a healthy and cheerful appearance.

Having thus told the reader what I saw, I will now detail my conversation with Madame Leclerc, in the course of which I asked her numerous questions, to which she gave me full and lucid answers, being a woman of strong and clear intelligence, who has evidently thought out many of the social problems connected with the manufacturing system.

Firstly, the hours of work are decidedly too long, according to our English feelings; but we must remember that it is not very long since Lord Shaftesbury gained his great battle, and reduced our working hours to ten. In France the rule appears to be twelve clear hours of labour. At this establishment the workpeople come at six in the morning and remain till ten, when they leave for the *dejeuner,* which is the great morning meal all over the Continent. They return at eleven, and work till three, when they again leave for dinner; the remaining hours are from four to eight. The day is thus evenly divided into thirds of four hours each, with one hour of intermission twice a day. In summer they come at five, and the *atelier* shuts at seven. Madame Leclerc assured me that the work never proved too much for the apprentices; and that sickly young people, accustomed to close, small rooms at home, often got healthy and blooming after a few weeks of regular work in these large airy *salles.*

The workmen, of whom there are 200, earn, when out of their apprenticeship, three francs a day. The workwomen, of whom there are 100, earn only half that sum. I asked the cause of the great difference, on which Monsieur Maitre said the labour of the men was really harder; but Madame Leclerc laughed, and said she thought it was custom more than any other cause which universally depressed the wages of women.

I asked if most of the women were married; she said yes, and that in the majority of instances the husbands were also in the *atelier.* If a man married, he usually asked work for his wife, and if any of the young women took a husband even from one of the neighbouring villages, it usually ended in his following her example, and entering the *atelier* of Monsieur Maitre. No workman or workwoman leading an immoral life is allowed to enter, and any culprit is immediately dismissed. Madame Leclerc spoke with the utmost decision on this point, and said that the moral condition of an *atelier* depended on the conduct and firmness of the master. No apprentice, boy or girl, is received until after they have made their *premiere communion,* and received a certificate that they can both read and write. The workpeople are thus of a respectable class.

I asked about the effect, upon the home, of the employment of the married women. Madame Leclerc answered that the young children were either sent out to nurse in the country, according to the very common custom of France, or else the married pair formed one household with the grandparents. She spoke of the latter arrangement as being of very general occurrence. *Toutefois* it was so managed that there was neither disorder nor discomfort at home. To which I could only reply, that they must be extraordinarily indebted to the genius of management possessed by the French people; to whom what we call "huggermugger" is apparently almost unknown. Madame Leclerc herself, though the mother of four children, regularly works with her father. Her husband was seated at a desk, which we passed in the course of our investigations, and her eldest little boy, of eight years old, leant against his mother's knee while she was talking to me. They live with Monsieur and Madame Maitre, the latter being now entirely out of the business, and devoted to the care of the household. The family of the *patron* thus exemplifies the arrangement carried out by a majority of his workpeople.

I think my readers will be interested in the printed rules of apprenticeship, which I translate as follows:—

"Article I.—Young people are admitted on the presentation of their relations, or, in default of these, by the persons who have adopted and are responsible for them.

"Article II.—They should be from thirteen to fifteen years of age; above and below this term the time of apprenticeship varies. In the first case it is longer, in the second shorter.

"Article III.—They will be required to prove, firstly, that they have received elementary instruction; secondly, that they have finished their religious education, and made their *premiire communion;* thirdly, they must be furnished with a medical certificate of vaccination.

"Article IV.—They will be admitted on trial for a fortnight; this time having elapsed, and without any other contract being drawn up, they will undertake, as also their relations or their guarantees, to execute with loyalty all the conditions stipulated, as follows:—

"terms Of Engagement. "Article V.—Young people from thirteen to fifteen years of age engage to remain two years and a half in the *ateliers* as apprentices. This time expired, a remission will be given them, and they will continue to be employed as workmen for as long as they may desire.

"Article VI.—If they wish to quit the *ateliers,* they must conform to the rule which requires them to give three months' warning before leaving; in consequence, any one who wishes to quit at the expiration of his apprenticeship, ought to give notice three months beforehand; and if they only do so on the day when the contract of apprenticeship expires, they will be obliged to work three months as workmen for wages before obtaining leave to quit.

"Article VII.—They will each receive, as a mark of encouragement, the sum of 425 francs (not quite £20), thus spread over the period:— / c.

During the first half-year 52
„ second „ 58 50
„ third „ 05
„ fourth „ 71 50
„ fifth „ 78

And at the expiration of the whole time 100

Total 425 0

"Article VIII.—Only the time actually passed in the *atelier* will be counted; thus any period lost by illness or any other cause of absence will not be reckoned, and they must complete the full two years and a half of apprenticeship.

"Article IX.—The apprentices must keep time exactly, and can absent themselves only after having obtained the authorization of the foreman *(amtremaUre)* of their *atelier.* They are required to obey the latter, as well as the workman specially charged with their instruction.

"Article X.—The apprentices who, without authority, shall leave the *atelier* before the expiration of their indentures, will be obliged to refund the following sums, namely: —the whole sum received during the first half-year; half of that received during the second half-year; and a third of that received during the third half-year. For the remaining period they will not be required to refund.

"Article XI.—Apprentices sent away for misconduct will be required to refund the same amount.

"Article XII.—In case of application of the two preceding articles, X. and XL, the parents or guardians of the young people will remain responsible for them, without prejudice to the responsibility incurred according to the law of the 4th of March, 1851, by the masters who may have consented to receive such apprentices into their *ateliers* 'The law of the 4th of March, 1851, is to the effect, that every master or workman convicted of having hired an apprentice from his employer, shall he chargeable for the whole or a part of the damages awarded to the master thus abandoned."

"GENERAL CONSIDERATIONS.

"The apprentices only enter the *atelier* to practise the different parts of the trade which they have adopted.

"These *ateliers* fulfil all the conditions desirable for guaranteeing the health of the young people; they are large, well kept, and possess light and air in abundance.

"The moral principles imposed by a firm exercise of authority, and recommended to them by good examples, are the surest warrant for the conduct of the apprentices.

"Their professional instruction will be carried out by initiation in good methods of work. In large and numerous *ateliers* neither lessons nor models can be wanting. They will be subjected to the happy influence of emulation, which will make them skilful and intelligent workpeople.

"Finally, they will not want for protection and paternal counsel; they will find both in their master, who will be always ready to encourage their efforts, and will have no other object than to form workmen able to make a position for themselves, and to do honour to his *atelier.*

"antoine Maitre."

I will conclude by the description of the *fete de I'Stablissement,* given me by Madame Leclerc with much enthusiasm. It is touching to see how completely her heart is in her work, and in the welfare of the people. On the 6th of May, the whole body of workpeople, accompanied by the Patron and his family, were accustomed to go to church together in the morning, returning to the atelier for a feast and a dance. They went *pele-mele* from their different houses, and were only imposing by their number; but two years ago Madame Leclerc, seized with the desire of making something pretty, and producing "*un bel effet,*" felt herself inspired with a bright idea, and said, "Father, why should we not go in procession!!!" So it was arranged. They placed the apprentices, boys and girls, first in order, who walked two and two. After these came the married couples arm in arm, accompanied by such of their children as were able to walk. The rear was brought up by Monsieur and Madame Matt re and their two young daughters, and Monsieur and Madame Leclerc with their children also. "Three hundred people walking to St. Benigne in procession! Ah! it was truly a beautiful sight!" said Madame Leclerc.

As I passed with her through the immense new *salles,* marvelling at the perfect order and organization of the whole, I asked if she thought 3000 workpeople could be as well organized and cared for as 300. She replied that she would not fear to undertake 3000, and that the condition of an atelier wholly depended on the masters; adding also, that where women were employed it was imperative to have a woman in some way employed in surveillance. She expressed the utmost astonishment that a lady could travel alone in a foreign country; and said she should be "quite bewildered," but laughed when I replied, "And I, Madam, should be quite bewildered if I were responsible for 300 workpeople and the organization of an establishment such as this."

"*Oh!*" said she, "*c'est Vhabitude, voila tout.*"'

A LEGEND OF BRITTANY.

TS it a farm or a castle?

The walls are of strong, grey stone, But the gate swings loose on its hinges, And a pillar is overthrown.
Desolate yawn the windows,
Never a one without flaw;
And the ample court of the chateau
    Is littered and strewn with straw.
    The oaken door in the portal,
    Where the children were wont to play, Stands open at noon and midnight,
    For the hall is choked with hay; And the stair which led to the chambers
    Is wholly unsafe to tread, Only the rats and the spiders
    Hold festival over head.
    The stalls for the hunting horses
    Are tenanted now by the cows, Over the Ladies' garden
    The lambs and their mothers browse;
At the well the windlass is broken,
    And whenever the beasts are dry, They drink 'midst the water-lilies,
    Of the Ladies' pond hard by.
    If you ask of the place its story,— It is not so far to seek;
It is fresh in the hearts of the people,
As if it had happened last week.
They talk of it often and often,
    As they smoke their pipes by the fire; And the youngest child in the household
    Could tell it the old grandsire.
    There were five fair sons at the table,
    When the lady was left to weep For the lord who lay in the chancel, Sleeping his last long sleep;
Five fair sons at the table,
    As pretty as boys may be,
When their mother was left a widow,
    With one little maid at her knee.
    But when, on a midnight of winter,
    Sad tidings were borne on the blast, And they knew in the north and the west
    That King Louis was murdered at last; The place of the lady was empty,
    In the chancel she slept with her lord,
And three of the boys she had nursed
    Crossed the Rhine with their musket and sword.
    But Herve, the gallant first-born,
    Who was gentle and good to the least; And Benigne, who was always his pride,
    For Benigne was a scholar and priest; And Renee, the flower of the flock,
    The maid with the beautiful hair,—

Benigne, in the zeal of his youth,
Half rebuked her for being so fair,—
Remained with the peasants they loved,
When darkness came down on the land, And the men who were born on the soil
Fought well under Herve's command; And the one tender maid of their race
Had two to protect her with care;
Herve by strength of his sword,
Benigne by the might of his prayer.
When Nantes, in the hands of the foe,
Ran red with the blood of her best;
The bands of the Terror went forth,
Fulfilling the Butcher's behest.
Then the moors to the north and the west,
And the woods of Count Herve's domain,
Were alight with the torches of war,
And ghastly with heaps of the slain.
There remained but a handful of men,
Who rushed to the feet of Benigne;
But Renee, the beautiful maid,
Ran forward, and flinging between,
Her voice full of passionate grief,
Yet with sweetness by anguish increased, "Oh! urge not to bloodshed," she cried,
"The sanctified hand of a priest *I*" "It is *I* who am left to defend My sire's castle,—away to the gate!
I will fight like a youth at the worst,
Like a man I will bow to my fate."
It was Renee who fell with her peasants,
Lying prone midst her beautiful hair;
'Twas Benigne who was struck on the threshold,
And died as he murmured a prayer.
And now, though the roofs be whole,
And the walls are of strong grey stone, There is not a man in the hamlet
Dare sleep in its chambers alone. And the farmer who owns the land,
With twilight is fain to go, And crosses himself with a thrill,
As he passes the old chateau.

THE HOME OF MADAME LOUISE. rjIHE life of Madame Louise, daughter of Louis XV., by the Abbe Proyard, published at Brussels in the year 1793, and translated and published in England in 1807, is an intensely interesting book,

well known, I have been told, to the older generation of Catholics, especially in Ireland; but I have never seen any reprint, and I doubt whether it exists in a more modern English dress than that of the oldfashioned edition " printed for the translator," and sold by J. Easton, of the High Street, Salisbury, and dedicated to Mary Christina, Lady Arundell. The book was lent to me by a Catholic friend many years before I had myself the happiness of being received into the Church, but it then made a deep, ineffaceable impression on my imagination, being the first picture ever brought before me of the beauty of a life of complete abnegation.

It happened in the year 1864 that, being in Paris, I was invited to attend a wedding in the town of St. Denis. The bridal party comprised some of my most intimate friends in France—all Catholics. I found the ceremony was to take place, not in the famous abbaye, which was and still is under repair, but in one of the parish churches, which had been at one time the chapel of the Carmelite Convent. Remembering whose memory was so vividly associated with the spot, I asked if any part of the convent yet stood, and was informed that the whole building existed as heretofore, but was converted into a barrack. And, iu fact, as we walked up the steps of the church, we saw soldiers' heads looking from the many windows of an old-fashioned building on the right-hand. Entrance was of course impossible, and I had to content myself with looking at the large wooden door which once led from the chapel into the adjacent house.

But about ten months ago, happening to pass a night at St. Denis, before leaving for Boulogne by a midday train, I went into the church in the morning, drawn thither, rather than to the abbaye, by the inexplicable attraction of Madame Louise. As I went up the steps, which are very numerous (for a reason afterwards to be explained), I noticed that the barrack was full of workmen, that some of the windows were unsashed, and the whole in a state of evident change. In the church, which was nearly empty, I observed a tablet of

black marble let into the wall above an official pew. I found it was to the memory of the Carmelite princess, and had a little postscript engraved at the end (down in the corner), to say that some one had saved this tablet in 1793, and that it had again been put up in 1817, when Madame Louise's nephew, Louis XVIII., was restored to the throne of his fathers. The inscription stated that her corpse had been interred in the chapter of the monastery. This made me determine to see something of the building, if possible, in spite of the masons and carpenters who held it in temporary possession. I went down several steps at the side of the church to a sort of antechamber of the sacristy, and in a little court adjoining saw three gentlemen busy over plans and drawings, and pointing to various parts of the masonry. They appeared to be surveyors, and I mustered courage to inquire of one of them which part of the edifice had been the home for so many years of the saintly and royal nun. Upon this the gentleman, who was elderly and grey-haired, went into a polite and benevolent ecstasy at the vivid interest displayed by an English Catholic in his country-woman, said that the whole block of buildings (which was truly immense) had been the Carmelite Convent, that it was now undergoing repairs, and that he would give instructions to one of his clerks to take me over it. This offer I gratefully accepted, and he then took me through the square in front of the church to an adjoining street, where opened the great gates and external court of the convent. The gates stood open, and the court was full of masons, blocks of stone, planks of wood, ladders," tools, and heaps of white dust. Here he handed me over to a bright lad of seventeen, who accepted the commission with gallant politeness, and took me into the interior of the vast house, through courts and cloisters, upstairs and downstairs, and over floors where half the planks were removed, talking volubly all the while about the past times of the convent, and with an enthusiasm for Madame Louise which I was rather astonished to find in one of his graceless age. He trotted me over a variety of abysses, regardless of my long years of seniority, and accepted *my* enthusiasm, expressed in doubtful French, as entirely due to the place and the occasion, and the proper complement to his *own*.

It was in April, 1770, that the Princess Louise, who had cherished since her early youth a secret longing to enter the religious life, went to the Carmelite Convent of St. Denis. The king, her father,—whose youngest and, perhaps, favourite child she was,—had given his permission in a letter so tender and touching, that one feels in the reading it what a strange mixture was the man and the monarch, who, blessed with a saintly wife and the best of sons and daughters, certainly loved and respected them with all that was good in his nature, and yet could not refrain from degrading vices, nor find strength in the pious emotions, of which he really appears to have been strongly susceptible, against weakness which held him up to public contempt.

We are told that, at the appointed day and hour, Madame Louise arrived at the Carmelites of St. Denis, accompanied by few persons. "The Superior received her at the outward gate, whilst the nuns, just informed of her coming, disposed themselves to receive her at the enclosure-door. She attended Mass in their chapel, which was in the interior of the house, and under that now used as a parish church; and after Mass, while Princess Louise stayed before the Blessed Sacrament, the Superior, as it was agreed, assembled the community in the parlour, and, without having prepared them in the least for such a piece of news, he (the Abbe Bertin) told them that the princess who had just entered their house, was no more to leave it, and that she was come only to be a Teresian. "

This convent was at the time in such distress that means no longer existed for providing the necessaries of life. The nuns "had for several years past made the most severe reductions-in their diet, already very frugal and scanty; they no longer drank any wine in the refectory; they ate but very little fish, and bought but the cheapest provisions; but notwithstanding their severe plan of economy, notwithstanding the generous assistance of Abbe Bertin and other charitable clergymen, the community, greatly involved in debt, could not satisfy their creditors. One day, the baker, for want of payment, refused to supply them with bread any longer; another time, a creditor signified to them a seizure of their revenues; in short, every day was marked by some fresh perplexity of distress, and the suppression of the house, which the nuns dreaded as their greatest misfortune, seemed unavoidable. The princess chose this house, which she did not know in the least, because she was informed that it was a very poor and regular community; and on this account she preferred it before all, avoiding the Convent of the Rue de Grenelle in Paris precisely because she was attached to it, and particularly acquainted with several of its nuns. "She also feared that, being situated in the capital, a residence there would expose her to receive many visits prejudicial to the spirit of solitude and retirement. Above all, it occurred to her mind that as they fired the guus as often as the king came to Paris, the noise would become for herself and her community an occasion of distraction at every visit the king would please to pay her." At the same time, her dutiful tenderness suggested a fear "whether the king would not have some repugnance to visit her in a place so near the grave of the kings of France; but as soon as this prince had assured her that he would see her there with as much pleasure as anywhere else, she instantly took her resolution to go to St. Denis."

As I crossed the threshold with my young guide, it seemed as if I were coming into the immediate presence of one so long familiar to my imagination. The memory of a holy life is an impregnating perfume which years have no power to destroy.

The chief part of the building runs round a large court with cloisters. It is an old-fashioned, many-windowed *corps de bdtiment*—such as meets the eye at every turn in Belgian towns, and in the more provincial parts of France. In the pillars of the cloisters, and in the inner walls, were several deep holes, from which the workmen had extracted metal hearts, each containing the *real* heart of some pious friend to the order. These would of course be restored, and I hope to the same niches; but I am sorry to say they were temporarily laid in a corner of the floor of the ancient oratory without sufficient protection from desecrating curiosity. The heart-shaped metal boxes were engraved with the name and titles of the dead, and a small tablet or *plaque* had been affixed to the wall outside each niche. Some of these inscriptions bore the names of Carmelite Sisters; others of great people of the world. I noticed particularly those of M. and Madame de Pomponne, dated 1745, and therefore the immediate descendants of Madame de Sevigne's friend, so frequently referred to in her letters.

In the oratory—a low vaulted apartment, looking out on a court where was once the convent garden—the walls were covered with half-effaced frescoes, representing the different occupations of the Carmelite day; and on the ceiling, painted to represent the sky, were little birds flying. Close to the oratory the workmen had dug deep down to the foundation of a small square apartment, probably another chapel, and they had laid bare the coffin of a sister: in several places the pavement was composed of funeral stones.

Then I was taken to the parlour, the kitchen, the *saJle* where the meditations were made. They were then empty, dusty, turned, as we should say, "upside down;" planks out of floors and ceilings, windows unglazed,—all the signs of active repair in progress. But in every one of these chambers dwelt the sweet and holy presence of the dead. It was in the kitchen that Madame Louise insisted on the meanest household drudgery, and that the king went with her to see supper cooked, and found to his surprise that the fire was only lighted an hour beforehand. "But as the Princess Louise assured him that she enjoyed better health than at Versailles, he concluded from thence that very likely the cold kitchen of the Carmelites was the most wholesome to her." It was in the refectory that she found herself to "have scruples at feeling so much pleasure in eating only beans and carrots," because her health, which had always been delicate amidst the fatiguing splendours of Versailles, actually improved amidst the rigours of Carmelite discipline. It was in the parlour that she consented to receive such visits as she could turn to profit for God; that she received a gentleman who had fallen into disgrace, and spoke to him "in so moving and Christian a manner, that when he left the monastery he cried out, 'I have forgotten all my misfortunes, since a holy princess has taught me so well how to support them profitably.'"

I was next taken up to see the long *dovtoirs,* but was told that Madame Louise had occupied a room which was now cut off from the rest of the building, and incorporated in an adjoining house, but that this room would eventually be restored to the rest of the convent; and then, with some difficulty, for the floors were in a dangerous state, and my young guide had to lay a plank across the open beams, I was taken into the infirmary where Madame Louise died. A week before my visit its state had been unchanged; but the under part of the floor was rotten, and the inlaid *parquet* had been taken up, and the grille of enclosure removed. The boy showed me where it had stood, fencing off the door through which the priest had entered to give her the last sacraments. When the repairs are executed, everything is to be replaced. Only the old-fashioned window yet remains untouched. I went up to and opened it; it looks across a small court to the wall of the present church. I thought of the "few days before her death, when she yielded to the entreaties of her sisters, and consented to sleep in the infirmary, and to break the abstinence prescribed by the rule; as for the rest, she followed as usual all the common exercises of the house." How, Thursday the 20th of December, she went to Mass and communicated, but had much difficulty to return from the choir; nevertheless, in the

evening she still would take her recreation with the nuns; and on Friday she passed the morning of the day as usual, and omitted none of her usual exercises of piety, but could no longer attend the recreation. It was on this day that she wrote a letter "to the king, my lord and nephew, to be sent to him after my death."

On the Saturday she "still took courage to get up," but could not go to the choir. On that day she recited her whole office, and she saw all her nuns as usual, and "answered all of them in words of wonderful edification and meekness." At seven o'clock that evening she invited the nuns who attended her "to recite with her the Litanies of our Blessed Lady." At eight she inquired if the hour of strict silence had not struck; having been answered in the affirmative, "Why did you not let me know it?" said she. "To be sick is not a privilege to break silence."

She lived eight hours longer; it was on the 23rd of December, at half-past four in the morning, that she passed away. Some are yet living who were infants then, for it is not quite eighty years ago. But what a different world is this we inhabit! As I stood with my hand on the hinge of that old French window, it seemed to me as if I stood within a sanctuary of the past, and were looking outwards into the ever-moving present. Yet this was a delusion; for the faith of Catholics and the rule of the Carmelite remain where they were—a sure refuge in a world of change.

It remains to be told that Madame Louise was buried in the ancient chapel *within* the house, with a tombstone built into the wall, and a niche where a lamp burnt perpetually. Traces of these yet remain; but when the new church was built (it was begun by Louis XVI., and raised above part of the old chapel, which accounts for the great flight of steps that have to be mounted from the Place), her coffin was removed to some vault constructed for it in connection with the later edifice. And now to what new inhabitants is this repaired convent to be given over? Are all the changes I have mentioned made for the benefit

of schoolboys, or schoolgirls, or hospital patients, or a regiment of zouaves, or a company of gendarmes? None of these. It is the Carmelite Sisters, who, after long years of absence, are coming to take possession of their home again! It is to be finished and refitted for them in eight months; and then the old order will be restored, the old prayers will resound once more, and the memory of Madame Louise will be honoured in the house where she so long dwelt.

LA ROSE DE SENS.

"ŒOSE de Sens, I saw you blooming
    By the grey cathedral door, When the shadows of the morning
    Fell athwart the marble floor; And the market women softly
    Up the pillared aisles did pass, With their caps as white as snowdrift,
    On their way to early Mass.
    But the pavement of the market
    Was alight with every hue, Which the darling flowers could muster,
    As they trimmed their lamps anew! 'Twas an early day in April
    When I bought the precious thing; But the beauty of the blossoms
    Made a summer of the spring!
    Rose de Sens, we bore you softly.
    As the sunnier days came on, Far from your native meadows,
    In the valley of the Yonne; From the turret, slim and dainty,
    Which the wheeling swallows haunt From the mighty massive minster,
    With its slow Gregorian chant;
    From the adamantine causeway,
    With its mosses overgrown; From the yellow, perfumed wallflower,
    Set in crannies of the stone; From the fragments of the ramparts,
    Half of Rome and half of Gaul, Which beat back the foes of Clovis
    From their vast embattled wall;
    From the poplars on the island,
    In the broad, unburdened stream, Where the English exile, Thomas,
    May have dreamed prophetic dream Of those distant Kentish meadows,
    Where, at scarce a later day, His own tomb should be the altar,
    Where half Europe flocked to pray. I have put you in my garden
    On the bills above the Seine, Where

many dainty roses

Drink their fill of summer rain; But whatever be their beauty,

Or how rare soe'er they be, There's not a rose among them

That can tell your tale to me!

THE DESERTED CHATEAU. JT was truly the summer of St. Martin, the day on which we took a long walk through the woods to the Chateau de Nerel. Our errand was very commonplace. The days were drawing short and cold, in spite of the brilliant beauty of the landscape, and we needed to lay in a stock of wood for winter firing. Now we had been told by our baker's wife, whose second son works up in the woods in the direction of Vaucresson, that a small farmer, renting land near the Chateau de Nerel, had some excellent wood on sale; *souches,* in fact, knotty roots of elm, such as would glow and sparkle charmingly in our open fireplaces, and not too dear. "Only fifteen francs, in fact, for a huge pile," said the baker's wife.

Up through the woods we went, till we reached a high plateau, where the trees had been felled within a year or two, and which commanded magnificent views to the south and west across the bright autumnal mosaic, to the long line of the aqueduct of Marly: grand reminiscence of Louis le Grand! It was the 5th of November—Gunpowder Plot, or what the French call " La Conspiration des Poudres,"— and the ground was strewed with gorgeous leaves. Little scarlet fungi grew on the mossy path; late sprigs of purple heather lingered amidst the underwood, and a solitary butterfly, half-stiffened by the cold, flapped his handsome wings feebly, as we lifted him out of danger on to a wayside branch.

Presently we came to the edge of the plateau, and saw the rich wooded vales which lie on the other side, and Yaucresson, with its white houses nestling amidst the groves, and the racecourse of La Marche, where all Paris rushes out to see " le sportfor we are not many miles away from Paris, though the country is so wild and beautiful. Royal power kept these tracts as chases for royal pleasures; and Nature, undisturbed, has

made them what she willed that they should be.

Just where the plain slopes to the valley, and ere yet the houses of the little town come in sight, we found ourselves skirting a broken wall; indeed a wall in such a state of dilapidation that here and there it ceased entirely for several yards; straggled bushes filled the gaps, and heaps of stone, overgrown with brambles, lay to the left of our path. Through the vacant spaces we saw what might have been taken for the ghost of a house;—tall, bare, with a highpitched roof, the upper windows mostly gone, these of the principal apartments yet filled with the small square panes of a century back, and opening down the middle with oldfashioned stateliness, though here and there a great hole proved that these rooms, too, were uninhabited.

On this south side or garden front, was no door, but the middle window came down to the ground; the scrubby grass of the field grew close up to the walls, and at a little distance began the fragment of an avenue, whose short, stumpy trees, lopped by some cruel hand, stretched down to a gateway, of which only one pillar remained, and which successive years had crowned with fantastic wreaths of ivy; while a pond, which had once been a piece of ornamental water, was half-choked with rushes. Precisely under this stunted avenue was the wood we had come to see, piled up in nice order,—the only neat thing about the place; and beside it stood a sharp, but pleasaut-visaged individual, clad in blouse and breeches of the universal blue, who expatiated on the special merits of his firewood, explaining that part of it was pure *eouche,* and the other part old scaffolding cut into lengths, and literally warranted as dry as a board.

Although I was equally to participate in the advantage of good fires, I had the bad manners to leave my companions to make their bargain without me; for that forlorn ghost of a house was more than the virtue of a reader of Anne Radclyffe could resist. It is my intimate conviction that old houses become sat-

urated with the spirit of successive generations; that their walls are not of mere brick or stone, but are interpenetrated, and become but the investiture of a mystic fabric; that of the home which the indwellers had made unto themselves.

You will say, my reader, that I am excusing my idleness and curiosity at the expense of some imagination; so I will confess that I picked my way over the rough grass of the field and round the corner in search of a door. At the side was the trace of a chapel pulled down in '93; at the back was the main entrance, a portal giving access to a hall or antechamber. This apartment filled the middle of the building, and through the opposite window I saw my companions bargaining over the wood-Up one side of the hall swept the graceful curve of a staircase, but the wall was half-destroyed, and the broad, shallow steps, broken in places, were littered with hay from an adjoining room which had been turned into a hay-loft. I mounted these steps with precaution, and reached a landing, with tall doors on either hand, and opened the one which led to the room above the hall, a large saloon with panelled walls and tall, narrow windows; a carpenter's bench on one side, and, huddled into a corner, an old armchair, which still retained shabby traces of gilding and blue satin damask.

I pushed through the rooms to the north wing, and came out on another staircase, much more perfect, which wound up in large spirals to the very top of the chateau. The architecture was unmistakably that of Louis XV.; a certain large proportion and air of antique grandeur, which characterizes all buildings of his reign; but emptiness reigned within as a visible presence.

"No human figure stirs to go or come;
Nor face looks out from shut or open casement;
No chimney smokes; there is no sign of home
From parapet to basement."

I ran up first to the top storey, where a long corridor connected a series of small attics in the high-pitched roof. In one of these was a broken-down bedstead; in another, a brown, tattered book lay on a broad window-sill. I took it up; it was a sort of army list of the First Empire. Descending to the next story, the rooms were much larger and loftier, and all panelled like those of the saloons; but several of the casements were out, and the rain had rotted the floors. Here and there the farmers had piled up their implements, planks of wood, and dirty sacks. I picked my way on this storey with some difficulty along the whole front of the house,—for all the rooms were *en suite,*—and from every window I saw M. Blouse Bleu, the pile of firewood, and my companions, who shouted to me as I leaned out of the empty sashes, and Henri ran round the corner of the chateau. At last I came to a door which was locked, and which resisted all my efforts to open it. It was at the angle, where the architecture slightly projected, so as to form a separate pavilion, though not sufficiently so to be called a tower. While I was shaking at this door, I heard the hollow sound of footsteps behind me, and Henri came tramping over the floors of the empty rooms. He took a deliberate shake of the door likewise, and then began to examine the lock. It was very old and very rusty; for a broken casement swung backwards and forwards close by. Henri took up a piece of iron which lay beside us, and in a moment the lock came off, and the tall door folded backwards into the room we desired to see. Here, to my intense surprise, we found furniture; complete, but very shabby fittings of fifty years back; small, faded squares of carpet on the *parquet,* which was solid, but utterly devoid of polish, and a table with a little gilt railing round the top; half a dozen chairs of black wood, a marble consol with gilt legs; a strange little mirror which had stared forlornly at the opposite wall for long, lonely years, and across which our own figures passing gave me a sudden thrill of surprise and fright. The fireplace was tidy; the pincers, the shovel, and a rotten old brush stood in the corner. On the high wooden chimney-piece were two bronze and gilt candlesticks,—femalo caryatides bearing on their heads two halfburnt wax-

candles, and between them a clock, surmounted by a little bronze figure of a soldier raising the eagles. The clock stood at half-past four.

Above the clock was a picture, which was neither hung nor nailed, but was painted on the panel itself, and formed part of the wall; and this picture inhabited the room; possessed itself of the faded furniture, gave a *raison d'etre* for the wide arm-chair which yet stood beside the grate, and was in its abundant vitality a witness of the cheerful family life which had once filled this melancholy old chateau. It was a portrait of a young man, a young officer of the First Empire, in the gay pompous dress which bore the visible stamp of the gay pompous Bonapartes of that day; it had a dash of Murat in it; *l'homme a l'oreille cassfa,* when he was a young fellow, had probably just that courageous and somewhat self-glorying smile; that head of thick, curly hair; that hat with the blue and white feathers; and this gay captain was painted in a somewhat singular attitude: in the act of kissing a farewell to one standing where we did,—beside the fireplace. About to join his regiment, which was just indicated in the back ground, the soldier was evidently walking away; but he turns round, he smiles at his darling, one hand holds a miniature to his lips, the other his plumed hat, which he is evidently about to wave. It is an adieu full of hope; full also of confident love. France has taken Germany and Italy with the sound of trumpets; she will take Russia on equally easy terms; the captain will become a general, a marshal of France; as plain as eyes can speak, those gay blue eyes look back and say, *"Adieu, ma bello cherie, mi revoir."* Under the picture was the name "Horace," and the date 1812.

We stood and gazed in silence, and Henri said softly,

"Ah! le pauvre Horace " "Who was he? what happened to him? why is he painted here? did he live in this Chateau"? I asked eagerly.

"No; he did not live here, but near Versailles; he was a captain under the First Empire; and what happened to him

was—never known."

"Never known!" cried I; "do you mean that he was a deserter?"

"No; said Henri, "le Capitaine Horace was no deserter, and to this day his name is frequently in the mouths of the older peasants in the neighbourhood, though between fifty and sixty years have gone by."

As Henri said this, we heard voices calling to us from the field below; and after vainly trying to unbar the window of the room in which we were standing, we went back into the adjoining one, and putting our heads through the aperture, we called to M. le Docteur and Marraine to come up; which they did; and I saw Marraine's eyes glisten with some strong emotion when she entered the closed room; while M. le Docteur hemmed in his throat, and said, "So *this* is the room about which my father used to tell us; but Marraine said, while she looked at the picture: "It is very like him;" for Marraine is eighty-five years old, and can remember the news of the king's death coming to the little village at the foot of the Pyrenees, where she was born, so that an event which happened only fifty-five years ago is comparatively recent to her.

"Ah!" said she; "I remember when this picture was painted, and the trouble it was to get it introduced into the Chateau; M. le Comte was no trifle, in those days, I can assure you, my dear; to be sure, poor man, he changed much before he died; *en effet,* the grief of Leonie was such that it conquered even his obstinacy, and it was M. le Comte himself who had the panel placed where you now see it."

This speech was addressed to the Doctor, who replied, "Ah, ah! poor dear! she lay in a bed placed against that wall opposite the fireplace, and my father said he could not persuade her to speak or to move till he tried the experiment of coming quickly into the room with a copy of the 'Moniteur' in his hand, and then she started up and clutched the paper frantically, and finding there nothing of what she wanted, broke into a wail of sobs and lamentations."

All this being to me quite unintelligible, I looked at Henri, who explained to me that Horace was the only son of a large army contractor under the First Empire; that he was a brave, gay, handsome young man, and had rapidly risen to be captain in the *grande armie.* That he had fallen in love with Leonie de Bausset, the only unmarried daughter of the then owner of this Chateau. The De Baussets were of old blood, but had returned from the emigration, and one of them occupied a place in the imperial household in 1812. Under his protection, the Comte, who still retained his Legitimist opinions, and would never take any post under Napoleon, was enabled to live in peace at the Chateau de Nerel. But he would not allow Leonie to become the wife of the son of an army contractor, however rich; and there had ensued the usual amount of pleadings, heart-broken love-letters, and paternal anger. Horace had been called away for the Russian campaign. Before he went, he caused this picture to be painted for his mistress, and it was kept by her carefully wrapped up in a piece of damask, and hidden away in one of the large cupboards found in the thick walls of these old houses. The young couple hoped for better times, and M. de Bausset, the cousin of Leonie, had promised to speak to the Emperor, and to get advancement for Horace; and so the girl saw her lover depart, with only the inevitable anxiety attaching to the ordinary chances of war. This was in the summer of 1812; and up to the first fortnight of October, Horace found means to write to Leonie with tolerable regularity. I *think* it was our Marraine who received his letter's, and gave them to Mdlle. de Bausset; but the dear old lady does not own to anything of the sort.

It was on the 7th of September that was fought the bloody battle of La Moskowa, or of Borodino, according to its Russian name. On the 15th was the famous entry into Moscow; on the 16th, Napoleon was driven out from the Kremlin by the conflagration which burst forth at once in various quarters of the city.

It was three days before he could return from the Chateau in the neighbourhood where he had taken refuge. The conflagration had then almost ceased, but about four-fifths of the city were destroyed, and in the remaining portion was sheltered the army of Napoleon, ransacking the ample cellars of the burnt houses for means of support. It is difficult to understand why a full month of that precious autumn weather should have been subsequently wasted at Moscow; grim winter was approaching, and the distance from France was something fearful to contemplate; yet it was not till the 19th of October that the *grande arrru'e,* 100,000 strong, marched from Moscow on the homeward road.

Horace was among those who thus started; man and beast well rested and fed with the "corn, salted meat, wine, brandy, sugar, and tea," which had been found in the cellars lodged for winter use. For some little time matters went on tolerably well; the regiments, the baggage wagons, the carts and carriages with women and children, even the troop of actors,—all the miscellaneous population which followed that great army in the assured hope of triumph,—filing in an immense line, many miles in length.

Then came on the great disaster. Intense cold set in, even earlier than might have been expected, late as was the season. The Russians harassed the retreating invaders with pitiless activity. The wretched peasants who had been burnt and starved out, retaliated with barbaric ferocity. Mistakes in generalship were committed; whole companies were caught in defiles, cut off from the main army, taken prisoners, slaughtered *en masse.* Many were fiendishly tortured by the peasants, according to the evidence of the English diplomatist, Sir Robert Wilson. Men dropped in the snow, and were left by their comrades miserably to perish; but one man was seen harnessed to the cart containing his sick wife; his horse had died of hardship, and the husband, substituting himself, actually dragged his wife leagues and leagues to a town where she could repose for awhile in safety. Another

man, an officer, was found sitting *dead* by a bivouac fire, the miniature of a fair young woman pressed to his stiffened lips. They buried him there and then, and laid the picture upon his breast between his crossed hands. His name was unknown—unregistered. Hundreds of officers perished namelessly, and men by the many thousand; who should take note of him? The soldier who dug the shallow grave in the chill morning, and who happened to survive and bring back the anecdote to France, said he was a fair man with curly hair, and the mother of Horace would always say it must have been her boy. But this story was kept from Leonie. Those who were about her thought it best to keep from her any piteous detail of cold and hunger upon which her imagination might fix itself, to the breaking of her poor burdened heart. As it was she heard only too much, for the awful fate of that immense army touched, by some link of relationship, almost every family in France; and when Napoleon, who had hurried back almost alone to Paris, before anyone knew that he was even approaching the capital, issued that famous and fatal 'Moniteur,' which was the first official and certain news of the catastrophe, it struck dismay far and wide over the country like the tolling of a great death-bell from the height of a cathedral tower.

It was by that number of the 'Moniteur' that the destruction of the army was known at the Chateau de Nercl; but not until the cessation of the letters of Horace had caused to the poor girl weeks of miserable watching and anxiety. But she dared say nothing in her family, only her father who was perfectly aware that Horace was in Russia, saw her fading and paling day by day. Then, when the issue of the fatal' Gazette' confirmed the worst fears of those at home in France, the old man was touched with a sort of pity.. Although the Chateau is not above eight miles from Paris, it lies on the verge of the royal woods in a somewhat out of the way situation, and the newspaper did not come there until the day after its ublication. But already the people at

Vaucresson knew what had happened; and one of the menservants who had ridden down to the little town in the afternoon, had come back and told the housekeeper that the Emperor had come home to the Tuileries, and that something dreadful had been published about the Russian retreat. She, poor woman, who knew very well how matters stood between Leonie and Horace, was sorely troubled, and she told her master that night what was talked about in the town. The Count made a bitter speech about the Emperor and relapsed into silence; but the next morning when the fatal 'Moniteur' came he hid it away, and went about all the morning with a grievous brow. If by any means he could have separated the two lovers, and married his daughter elsewhere, he would only too gladly have done it. But in *this* manner of gaining his end there was something too dreadful; and the heart of the nation was too deeply moved by the national misfortune for the old man not to feel for sorrow which fell upon his household from that source.

In the afternoon, Leonie, who had been peculiarly restless that day, saw from her window the Cure of Vaucresson walking up the avenue. She descended quickly, for the old man was a friend, and she loved him. She met him in the hall, just as the Count himself came in from the garden by the other door. He tried to make a gesture of warning; but too late. The Cure, absorbed by the terrible news,—he had had a brother high in command in that lost army,—came hurrying into the house, the tears streaming from his aged eyes, the 'Moniteur' in his hand. "Ah! M. le Comte; ah, my dear friend! my brother, my poor Victor,—I shall never see him more; and his widow, and my poor little nieces,—my Rosalie, my Hortense " The Cure stopped; for Leonie, clutching desperately at the 'Gazette,' had cast a hasty glance at the bulletin, and fel) senseless upon the marble floor.

They lifted her up; they carried her into her room, and laid her on her bed, her hand still holding the 'Moniteur' in its icy grasp. For three days they could not get her to speak a word, nor would she take food or wine except by compulsion from her father. Then the Cure, to whom the story was told, went to Versailles, and implored the mother of Horace to come and see the stricken girl. In the depth of her own distress, the poor lady yet came over, and by her stronger nature and firmer faith she brought Leonie to something like submission. But the spring was broken, and though Mdlle. de Bausset lived many years, it was as a changed woman, and gradually, after her father's death, as a complete recluse. It was her father who, thinking to give her some consolation, actually gave the order for the portrait of Horace being attached to the panelling of the room. In ten or twelve years the old Comte died, leaving the Chateau to Leonie, with a strong recommendation to his sons so to arrange the division of the property as to allow their sister to keep her home. It was done, and Leonie dwelt on there until the year 1847. She was then fifty-three, and for twenty years she had never left the grounds; for the last five she had remained wholly in her room, though no apparent malady preyed upon her.

Even during her lifetime the chief rooms of the Chateau fell into much decay. She seemed to care for nothing, and would repair neither decorations nor furniture, nor renew the rich hangings as they faded by lapse of years. And when at length she died, and the brothers sold the property, no one cared to refit the old mansion; the farmers used it for their grains and implements; the wind and the weather came whistling through the broken panes; the unmended roof caused further mischief; the grounds became a desolate wilderness; the avenue was not replanted when the old trees were cut down for firewood. The persistent grief of Mdlle. de Bausset, and the long, long years through which her young life had wasted itself away, had impressed the imagination of the neighbourhood. They said at last that the place was haunted, and that the pale grey forms of the officer and his betrothed were seen wandering in the plantations at dusk, and standing by the weedy pond, looking down upon the strangled water-lilies.

Henri told me this story while we stood in the closed room-, looking tearfully at one another. Marianne shook her head mournfully, with its great bows of white hair framing her handsome aquiline old face. She would not own to having carried those love-letters fifty-five long years ago (but I am sure it was she). She only said, "Ah! we never told *her,* but his mother and I always thought that it was our poor Horace who was found one ice-cold morning, with the miniature pressed to his dead lips, by the embers of the bivouac fire." THE CURE OF TLOERMEL.

TUST ere the stroke of midnight fell,
The ancient priest of Ploermel Sat by his fire one Christmas night. Still as the grave the frosty air,— His lips were murmuring a prayer, The while his heart was softly moved With thoughts of many a youth he loved In college days, at peaceful Vannes, Beside the Sea of Morbihan. Now some were old and far away, And some had spent their little day In wondrous Paris on the Seine; And some amidst the stormy main Which sweeps round Brittany were lost; Thinking of such, his brow he crossed, And bowed the head whose locks were white.

Sudden, amidst the hush profound,
The far faint echo of a sound
Stole to his ear; 'twas such as springs
From the slow beat of countless wings,
Or rustle of a multitude
That softly pace a moss-grown wood.
Noiseless he crossed his earthen floor,
And looked into the silvery light
Along the road which passed his door,
And saw,—a strange and awful sight!
Far as his aged eyes could reach,—
With sound of neither tread nor speech,—
Stretched the long files of grey and white.
All silent in the moonshine went
Each cloaked and hooded penitent,
Bearing a torch which burnt upright.
The trembling Cure made the Sign;
Each phantom bent in grave incline,
As when the wind of summer sweet
Bows all the rippling ranks of wheat!

The foremost, as he passed the door,
Motioned the Cure on before,
Who mute obeyed; some ghostly spell
Moved the good priest of Ploermel.
And so the mighty multitude,
Across the moor and through the wood,
    Followed, yet guided him, until
    His feet by that same spell stood still
    Before the open porch, which yet
    In a long roofless wall was set.
    The ruined church was one which
long
    Had only heard the night bird's song,
    But still the altar-steps were there,
    And a wild rose in festoons fair
    Graced it in summer; now the fern
    And ivy draped it in their turn.
    Then all that mighty multitude
    Within the vast enclosure stood,
    The moonlight on their garments
shone,
    And still their torches burned; whilst
one
    Mounted the mossy steps, and took
    Stained vestments and an ancient
book,
    And old chased chalice from the
stone.
    With silent awe the saintly priest
    Robed for the wonted Christmas
feast;
    And every shrouded penitent
    On humble knees devoutly bent,
    One served the Mass, and all intent
    Responded with the mystic tone
    Of winds and waves together blent.
    But when he raised the sacred Host
    The vague uncertain tone was lost
    In sweetest music of the upper
spheres;
And when the Cure raised his hand and
blest
The kneeling flock, with *Ite, missa est,*
The shrouded penitents were seen to
softly rise
Like a white shining cloud to his aston-
ished eyes
And ere the last sweet gospel words
were done,
The nave was empty,—the good priest
alone
Invoked the Father, Son, and Holy
Ghost;
While from the distant skies a heavenly
host

Of souls set free from purgatorial pain,
Sang as they took their flight, the sweet
refrain,
"Hath been, is now, and ever more shall
be,
World without end! Amen I"
THE AGE OF ST. LOUIS.

rjIHE traveller in France, who cares to
investigate her history and antiquities,
cannot go many miles without being arrested by some trace of that vigorous
epoch, so prolific in beauty,—the thirteenth century. And what he finds of
most beautiful, of most enduring, is sure
to be in some manner associated with
the man who was the verytype of that
age,—St. Louis of France; King Louis,
the saintly soul, the wise and honest
ruler, the gallant Crusader, who died of
fever on the plain of Carthage, and
whose loss was so bitterly deplored by
his old friend and chronicler, de
Joinville, that he accuses all those who
counselled or abetted that last crusade
as guilty of mortal sin.
St. Louis is one of the great men of
whom history has told us many little
private details, and it is these which fa-
miliarize a hero in the imagination of
succeeding ages. That one dear friend
and fellow-soldier,—the Seneschal of
Champagne,—who went with him during the seven long years of his first Crusade,—long outlived the king, attaining
the extreme age of ninety-five. It was
in the month of October, 1309, that the
Seneschal, who was at that time eighty-
five years old, undertook to put together
what he could personally remember of
St. Louis, who had then been dead nearly forty years. And a very quaint, living
chronicle he made; which would naturally be now quite unreadable, by reason of the different spelling, but which
has been so far modernized as to be
comprehensible, and was so published
in 1853 by the Abbe Millault, Superieur
du Petit Seminaire de Paris. Only the
spelling appears to have been changed,
as the diction is quite medieval, and a
short glossary has been added at the
end.
    Firstly, as to De Joinville himself. He
was of a great family; his mother was
first cousin to the German Emperor,

Frederick II., and he himself descended
from other Sires de Joinville, who had
followed successive monarcha in the
Holy Wars. He was yet very young
when his father died, and was brought
up at the provincial court of Provins and
Troyes, which was the most polished of
that age. Here the young Joinville acquired that elegance of manner which
afterwards caused him to be sought in
the courts of the kings of France. When
his legitimate chief, Count Thibaut, the
fourth of Champagne, went to the Crusades in 1238, Joinville, who was barely
fifteen, was obliged to stay at home; but
he was shortly after knighted, and in
due season married Alix de Grandpre,
cousin to the Comte de Soissons. When
Thibaut came back from the Holy War,
he made the young Chevalier Seneschal
of Champagne, as his father had been
before him.
    When Louis IX. se *croisait,* as the ex-
pression was, the chivalry of Champagne flocked to his standard, and De
Joiuville, though a young man only four
or five years married, did not hesitate
to take arms. His mother was yet living,
and possessed his father's estate, so that
he had much ado to get the money for
the ten knights whom he took with him,
each of whom had squires and servants
belonging to them, all of whom were at
the expense of the lord.
    "At Easter," says he, "in the year of
grace 1248, I sent for my men and vassals to Joinville, and on Easter Eve,
when all these people had come, was
born my son John Sire d'Ancerille, of
my first wife, who was sister of the
Comte de Grandpre. All that week we
were in the midst of feasts and ban-
quets, for my brother, the Sire de Van-
couleurs, and the other rich men who
were there, provided meats one after the
other, on the Monday, Tuesday, Wednesday, and Thursday.
    "On the Friday I said to them, ' My
lords, I am going beyond seas, and I do
not know if I shall come back. Tell me,
therefore, if I have done you wrong in
any matter; I will repair it at all points,
as I am accustomed to do by those who
come to require somewhat from me or
from my people.' This I did according

to the opinion of those who belonged to my estate, and that they might have nought against me, I held myself apart while they held counsel together; and executed without delay all their decisions.

"On the day when I left Joinville, I sent to ask for the Abbe de Cheminon, who was reputed the wisest man of the White Order.... This Abbe de Cheminon invested me with the scarf and belt, and then I left Joinville without again entering the Chateau, until my return (from the Holy War). 1 left with bare feet, and clad in a shirt, and so I went to Blecourt and to Saint-Urbain and to other holy relics which are there; and while I went to Blecourt and to SaintUrbain, I would never turn my eyes again towards Joinville, for fear my heart should melt at the sight of the fair Chateau which I was leaving, and at the thought of my two children."

So went De Joinville forth from his home, and ate his first meal at Fontaine l'Archeveque, about five miles on his route. Then from Auxonne he travelled on to Lyons, and descended the Saone in boats,—the chargers being led along the river side. At Lyons he took the Rhone, and mentions that he passed a castle called Roche de Gluy, which the king had caused to be pulled down, because Roger, the lord thereof, had robbed pilgrims and merchants. It was not s long ere De JoinviUe reached Marseilles, and embarked on that perilous Mediterranean, which not even all the resources of modern navigation can prevent from causing constant destruction. Only last year a large steamer left Marseilles for Algiers, and was never heard of more; and another was cast upon the shore near Oran, with a frightful loss of life. What, then, must have been the risk to these French Crusaders, never a maritime people, setting off within their thirteenth-century vessels to traverse the whole length of the Mediterranean from west to east, with the " Saracens of Barbary" ready to devour them, if they got a chance, by sea or land, and all manner of rocks and islets, and ugly stories and dire traditions,— half classical, half Christian,— sur-

rounding their onward track! The unhappy horses were put into some sheltered hold, and the door was fastened upon them; "just," De Joinville observes, "as one would cork the bunghole of a barrel which one is putting into the water, because, when the ship is at sea, the door would be in the water. " Then the pilot cried out to those in the prow, "Are you all ready?" "Yes," they replied. "Let the clerks and priests come forward then," replied the pilot, and when they were come, he said, " Sing in the name of God;" and they fell to chanting, "Veni, Creator Spiritus," from beginning to end; and the pilot cried out to the sailors, "Set sail, in the name of God." And then the sails filled, and the vessel presently lost sight of land. And that was how the Crusaders left France for the Holy Land. Says De Joinville, " Every day the wind bore us further from the country where we were born; and by that I would have you to see that he is a hardy fool who would dare to put himself in such peril with other people's goods, or in a state of mortal sin; for one goes to sleep of a night, and one knows not whether by morning one may not find oneself at the bottom of the sea."

When they had gone some way, they came to an island which was to their imagination "quite round for it was the hour of Vespers when they arrived, and after sailing all night, and making, as they thought, about 150 miles, they found themselves still in front of this same island; and this happened two or three times, so that they thought the place must be bewitched, and made a solemn procession, with prayers, round the two masts of the vessel; De Joinville being so ill that he had to be held up by the arms. After this they lost sight of the mountainous isle, and reached Cyprus in safety. At Cyprus they found the king, and also an immense quantity of provisions, which had been laid in during two previous years, innumerable tons of wine, and such a quantity of corn and grain, piled up in heaps in the fields, that the outside, having been rained upon, had sprouted, and looked like green grass. But when the crust was removed,

the grain was found underneath as fresh as if recently threshed.

Now this is no "place for recounting the history of the seven years' Crusade, through which Dc Joinville adhered faithfully to St. Louis. When they at last came back to France, he returned with them, and went home to Champagne. The people on his estate had suffered much during his absence; they flocked to address their complaints to him, and conjured him not to leave them again. And their tears, and the knowledge of their misfortunes made such an impression on the Seneschal that he would not consent to leave them a second time, in spite of the urgent instances of St. Louis himself.

He went, however, many times to Paris, and every time that the king saw his faithful comrade of the Holy War, he made such rejoicing that everybody about him was astonished. The pious gravity of St. Louis was enlivened by the gayer spirit of De Joinville, and they were ever close friends and companions.

All the time when he was not at the court of the King of France or of the Count of Champagne, the Seneschal passed among his vassals. Ho visited the sick and helped the poor, and built and repaired churches, and in the midst of his labours the scenes beyond seas were not forgotten, for he caused to be painted several incidents from the Holy War upon the glass windows of his chapel at Joinville, and of the church of Blecourt.

This is an example of the individuality of the architecture of the thirteenth century; of the way in which the founders or restorers of churches built their experience into that which they created; so that the names and destinations of the sacred edifices and the various decorations and the tombs and inscriptions which they contain, all tell living tales of the people of that generation.

Many years had passed since the return from the East, when St. Louis sent for all his barons to come to Paris during Lent. De Joinville was ill, and excused himself; but the king replied, that he had good physicians at Paris, who could cure quartan fever, and that, in fact, come De Joinville must. So to Paris the Seneschal went, arriving on the 24th of March, 1269, but could not learn why the king should have so urgently required his presence. At Matins, the next morning, or rather in the night, De Joinville went to sleep and had a dream, in which he saw the king kneeling before an altar and surrounded by priests, who covered him with a scarlet chasuble. Thereupon he consulted Monseigneur Guillaume, a very wise priest, and told him of this vision; and to his extreme dismay the holy man replied, that in his opinion it meant that the king was again going to the Crusades, "Sire, vous verrez que le Roi se croisera demain." And so it proved.

And this resolution was indeed a sad one for France, and worse than even the subjects of the saintly king expected; many years had he been absent on the occasion of the last Crusade, but from this one he returned no more. And De Joinville, when much pressed by St. Louis and the King of Navarre to accompany them, replied, that while he had been beyond seas before in the service of God and the king, and since his return, the sub-officers had injured his people and impoverished his estate, so that there would never be an hour in his life but that the injury would be felt. "And I told them, also, that if I desired to do the will of God in the matter I should stay here to hold and to defend my people. For if I put my body to the venture of the pilgrimage of the Cross, I saw quite clearly that it would be for the misfortune and harm of my vassals and against the will of God, who gave His own body to save His people.

"Indeed I think that all those who had advised the king to go as a Crusader committed mortal sin; because so long as he was in France all the kingdom kept good peace with itself and with its neighbours, but since he went away the country became unhappy. And also great sin had they who advised him to go, because of the great weakness of his body; for he could neither bear to be conveyed in a carriage, nor to ride

a horse; and feeble as he was, perhaps, if he had remained in France, he might still have lived on *(assez),* and would have done much good."

So De Joinville remained at home, minding his vassals, and was not with the king when he died upon the plain of Carthage; but when the corpse was brought back to France and laid in a tomb at St. Denis, and the Pope commissioned the Archbishop of Rouen and Frere Jean de Samoys, afterwards a bishop, to go to St. Denis, and to make lengthened inquiry concerning the life, the works, and the alleged miracles of the holy king; Joinville was sent for to Rouen to appear as a witness, and was detained two days. And when his testimony and that of many others had been duly sworn, and the results taken before the authorities at Rome, the Pope named King Louis as one of the Confessors of the Church, to the great glory and joy of his kingdom of France. And the Seneschal had a dream that he beheld the new Confessor before his own chapel at Joinville, who seemed marvellously joyous and full of heart's ease, and the ancient comrade and subject was likewise joyous at seeing him there; "and said, 'Sire, when you leave here I will lodge you in my house in my town named Chavillon.' And he answered me gently, 'Sire de Joinville, by the faith which I owe you, I do not think to leave this so soon.'"

Then Joinville, when he awoke, fell to thinking, and interpreted his dream as a sign that he should raise an altar in that very chapel to the honour of God, under the mediation of Louis the Confessor. Which he did, and established a perpetual endowment for the serving of the same. And Joinville recounting this, adds a delicate observation to the effect that Monseigneur le Roi Louis, great-grandson of the Confessor, who was on the throne at the time of the writing of the memoirs, knew of the said altar, and would do a kind and laudable action, if he would send some relics of the body of St. Louis to Joinville, to inflame the devotion of the worshippers.

Nothing more is known of the life of the aged Seneschal, who remained

for several generations a living testimony to the worth of his early friend and master. At last, when he was eighty-five years old, Queen Jeanne de Navarre begged him to write down all he remembered; to which request we owe these famous memoirs of St. Louis. He was ninety-five when he died, having seen five reigns; his son John, who was born to him in his youth when he was about to start for the Holy Land, died long before him. His second son, Anselme, succeeded him as Seneschal of Champagne. The only son of Anselme had no male heir, and thus was extinguished the ancient race of the Sires de Joinville. The lordship passed into the family of the Guises, and later into that of Orleans. The exiled Prince de Joinville now keeps up the name of the friend of St. Louis.

The Seneschal was buried in the church of Saint-Lament, close to his castle. Above the vault a simple tomb had been raised—in the choir; on it he was represented in his old age, clad in a coat of mail which fell to his knees. His epitaph, written in Latin, contained two important dates— the year in which Jehan sire de Joinville was born, 1224; and the year in which he died, 1319. This tomb was respected until the great Revolution; and in 1793, at the same time that the royal tombs at St. Denis were profaned, and the ashes of St. Louis scattered to the winds, the grave of his faithful friend, the Seneschal, shared the same fate. But the inhabitants of the little city of Joinville rose at the sight of this profanation, and obliged the local authorities to gather up and re-inter the remains of the sires of Joinville and Princes of Lorraine in the cemetery of the town, where they still lie without any monument to mark the place. The church of St. Lament no longer exists, and all its monuments are destroyed or displaced. As early as the year 1790, the buildings of the Chateau had been sold on condition that they should be destroyed. This condition has been but too well fulfilled; pines and poplars now cover the hill where reared itself the beautiful Chateau which the Lord of Joinville, parting for the Holy War, did not dare to look back upon, for fear his heart should fail him!

THE LAST CRUSADER.

JpAR across the waste of waters,
  Lashed by fierce Homeric gales, Is a land of famous story,
  Lying southward of Marseilles. But three thousand years have crumbled
  Into dust her ancient pride; 'Twas amidst her ruined temples
  That the last Crusader died.
  For " Delenda est Carthago"
  Was the threat proclaimed of yore;
And upon her waves triumphant
  White-winged vessels ride no more.
Heaps of stone, o'ergrown with brambles, Mutely eloquent, attest
That the race which called her mother,
  Sleep forgotten on her breast.
  And a troop of slow-paced Arabs,
Passing in a silent file,
Fix the eye which else would vainly
Range the plain from mile to mile.
Not a dwelling known to Carthage!
Not one altar on the hill!
Empty lie her land-locked harbours,
  Margins bare, and waters still!
  Empty graves through which the hyena
  Ranges, laughing at decay, Strike their dark and dangerous labyrinth
  Inward from the light of day. And such utter desolation
  Triumphs here, it may be said, That of this forgotten nation,
  Even the graves give up their dead!
  On which summit was the Byrsa
Scipio fought five days to gain!
  Here is nought but what the footsteps
In five minutes might attain.
  Can it be that once a million
People dwelt upon this plain?
But for us this shore is haunted
  By the phantoms of our own; All amidst its desolation
  The best blood of France is sown.
Through the bramble and the blossom
  Springs the historic Fleur-de-Lys;
And we hear the self-same requiem
  Which they chant at St. Denis!
  Ah! his sacred grave is rifled; Scattered wide his sainted dust,
But his name has still its fragrance
As the memory of the just.
And his France has not forgotten
To record on yon hillside,
That the greatest of her monarchs
  On the shore of Carthage died.

COASTING ON THE MEDITERRANEAN. JN looking over these records of French travel, I have felt that my book would be incomplete, as a record of personal experience, without some mention of the many happy days spent on board the great French steamers, most of them belonging to the Messageries Imperiales, which sweep the historic waters of the Mediterranean, from site to site now under the rule of France. I have stood on the deck of one of these great vessels, on a day when sky and water were both of calm cloudless blue, watching the long stretch of dream-like country between Marseilles and Nice; passing Hyeres, where St. Louis disembarked on his return from his long Crusade, having with difficulty consented not to go on by sea to Aigues Mortes, because De Joinville, his faithful counsellor, reminded him of what had happened to Madame de Bourbon; namely, that she had re-embarked from this very port of Hyeres, and had been driven about by wind and weather for seven weeks! But in *our* vessel, 800 years later, we escaped with only one day's delay; for having quitted the last sunny belt of southern France, and passed Spezzia and Livorno, such a storm arose on that treacherous water, that even the modern steamer was forced to lie-to in the port of San Stefano, and there all the company, French, Irish, and English, were kept fretting and fuming for four-and-twenty hours, not exactly in danger of life and limb, but suffering from a grievous want of fresh milk for their tea and coffee.

And I have also been twice across the Mediterranean to Algiers, that strange colony where the east and the west mingle together in a fantastic union, which must be seen to be believed—the colony which is only two days' journey from Marseilles, but where the Patriarchs stalk sublimely through the ravines and across the sandy plains covered with the dwarf palm, while the tricolour floats on every public building; and the Sisters of Charity walk quietly along in their white cornettes, with their long gowns of blue serge tucked up under their string of beads, and the veiled Moorish women shuffle along, with two black eyes peeping out of a slit, and their slippers down at heel!

Of the French conquest of Algiers, begun in the last days of old Bourbon rule, and carried on by a series of splendid victories under the government of Louis Philippe,—is it not all painted by Horace Vernet, and hung up in the great national gallery of Versailles! And of French efforts at colonization, and of the local authorities, and of the diocese of Algiers, with its religious pioneers seeking to reconstitute the ancient famous Church of Africa; of the martyrdom of the convert Geronymo in the sixteenth century; of the find-ing, within the last twenty years, of his *masque* in the plaster wall of the strong old fort where he had been built up alive;—of all this what might not be written? But Algiers and the French are an old subject now. So much has been put forth by English winter residents that the picturesque story lacks freshness; and though, at the time, I wrote several papers, it is hardly worth while to reprint them here. But it so happened that in leaving the colony for Rome, in the spring of 1857, I took a very unusual route; coasting along the whole eastern province of Constantine, and stopping for two days at Tunis, which is celebrated in the ancient annals of France, as the place where St. Louis died on his way to his last Crusade. On a hill some miles from Tunis, and overlooking the desolate plain of ancient Carthage, is the small piece of land given by the Bey to France, and on it is erected a memorial chapel served by a French priest. The surrounding country is still what it must have been in 1270. Centuries count for little in this part of the world. The same low white, flat-roofed Moorish town; the same immense lovely bay and jagged mountains, the same rocky, uneven, shrub and flower-grown plain,— where once stood Carthage! I will tell what I saw in the words which I wrote at the time; and then relate, in the words of the old chronicler, what took place at Carthage 800 years ago.

How many people of mature years, having read the Roman history in their youth, and having carried away from that austere field of learning many noble legends, and not a few theories of social life, have any clear idea of what they would see if they went to the site of the city of Hannibal?

A general impression appears to exist that the very place of its foundation is uncertain, and that all vestiges of the great maritime metropolis of antiquity have passed away. Nineveh has rendered up her tale of burnt bricks; and the gigantic basements of the temples of Baalbec are still an inscrutable amazement to modern engineers. To the traveller who stumbles amidst the forest tracks of Central America, the richly sculptured monuments of Mexico record a primeval civilization, whose lineage is unknown. Thebes and Memphis yet rear their massive columns from out the drifted sand. Rome has her Mamertine prisons, half built, half scooped from the living rock; her Cloaca Maxima, her Servian ramparts, yet attest the public spirit of the early Tarquins; and torches let down into the foundations of the Capitol reveal the huge steps of that secret staircase, trod by senatorial feet two thousand years ago. The Parthenon, now shattered in its fair proportions, stood nearly perfect on the Acropolis, until the century before last. Not until 1087, when it was used as a powder-magazine by the Turks, at the time of the city being besieged by the Venetians, could the temple of Pericles and the shrine of Minerva be said to be fairly ruined. But Carthage, which was a great city when Rome was but a herdsman's village; Carthage, the daughter of Phoenicia, whose lineage stretches back into the dim morning twilight of time; Carthage the wealthy, the ambitious, the luxurious, she who sent out armies to the fields, and galleys to the great waters, and whose founder was a priestess-queen,—what is she now? I will tell you, for I have seen her,—a wide grassy plain, slightly raised above the level of the blue Mediterranean; an uneven, desolate, dangerous plain, covered for

miles with lumps of ruin, mere cairns of stone tumbled together, where the traveller must pick his way with heedful steps, lest he fall unawares into some yawning chasm, the cellar or the water-cistern of a Carthaginian house; or, perchance, the very dwelling itself, lying far beneath the level of the accumulated soil; a mere gulf of blackness and death to the unwary. And this is Carthage!

I had come from Algiers, coasting eastward along the north of Africa in a French steamer, which stayed some hours at each principal port, at Bougia, at Philippeville, at Bona, and finally at Tunis. The steamer was advertised to T leave Algiers on Tuesday, the 10th of March, but the Mediterranean had lashed itself up into such a state of fury that the captain did not dare put forth. In twenty-four hours the sea, though still running heavily, had so far subsided that we started; but what occurred during the next twelve hours deponent saith not, being only able to cast occasional hurried glances at the mountainous borders of Kabylia, their snowy tops seen through the driving mist. Much of Kabylia is still unconquered by the French, though lying in the very heart of the colony; its rocky fastnesses protect its warlike mountaineers, who boast themselves the aboriginal unsubjugated race, whom neither Roman, nor fiery Arabian Moor, nor glory-loving son of Gaul, have yet enslaved beneath their yoke. The Kabyles are, in many respects, the best of what may now be roughly termed the native races. They congregate in villages, and do not live a nomade life. They dwell more in huts than in tents; and they display a remarkable aptitude for handicrafts and manufactures, fashioning, and even engraving gun-stocks and barrels, for they are workers in metals, like Tubal Cain of old.

Early on Thursday morning we had left the shores of their territory,.and landed at Bougia, once a large Roman city, and still retaining, in its fragments of massive wall and one perfect arch, the trace of Roman occupation. A great many monkeys are said to inhabit the hills at the back of the town, and we saw

two tame ones playing in the garden of a private house. Midday we steamed off again; and at dawn on Friday found ourselves at Stora, the little port of Philippeville. The latter town lies also at the water's edge, some three miles off; but, for some reason, it is not safe for boats to run up to it. It has never been a Moorish, but was once a Roman, site. There are immense cisterns high up behind the town, which have been roofed in by the French, and restored to full efficiency. There is also a fragmentary amphitheatre, whose stone seats and semicircular wall form part of the playground of a boys' school; and before the church stands the statue of an imperial Caesar, nameless and noseless, but supposed to be Hadrian. Every relic of antiquity possessing real interest has been sent off to France.

At Philippeville I had to remain nearly two days, for the steamer goes no further; if I remember rightly, it turned north for Marseilles; but on Saturday came another, which started in the evening for Bona; for the plan of Mediterranean steam communication is always that the vessels travel by night, halting by day to pick up passengers and merchandise, and to unload stores; as, of course, all the luxuries, and many of the necessaries of life are brought from France. I remember how red the sunset was that night over those wild African hills, the richness of the wayside flowers, as the kind consul drove me himself to Stora by a road that wound close to the edge of the beautiful bay.

At Bona, next morning, there was plenty of bustle, Sunday though it were. There is a large Arab population, and it seemed to be market-day for them outside the town. Inside the bells were ringing for early Mass, and all the French were abroad. One of the ship's officers, a certain M. Pijon, who had travelled in the East the year before with Mr. Holman Hunt, very kindly took me on shore to see the long line of a Roman aqueduct at the back of the town.

We passed a large party of bare-legged creatures in bernouses, chaffering round a sorry white horse, which was "going, going, *gone,*" for a sum of money equivalent to £5; others were buying and selling edibles, and all the strange bodily gear in which half-savage nations delight,— articles made of leather and cord, and coarse coloured cloth, of such shapes and sizes as no European could invent for a price. As a dead contrast, I remember trying to find some readable literature in Bona, to while away the many days of sea-travel that yet lay between me and Italy, and that I could get nothing but immense, yellow, double-columned French novels, with pictures of very fine gentlemen on their despairing knees to very fine ladies in Parisian *salon.* It was at that wild and wonderful Bona, on a Sabbath morning,—the clear chime of the Catholic bells rising above the Arab clamour,—that I came across 'Marguerite, ou les Deux Amours/ by the fair and witty Delphine Gay, the Corinne of France, afterwards Madame de Girardin; this was a story of a fair young lady who was sought in marriage by two equally devoted lovers, and who, reversing the sad plight of Captain Macheath in the 'Beggar's Opera/—

"Could be happy with *neither* away;" and being finally married by the most obstinate of the two, heard that the deserted man had shot himself, and died *herself* on her wedding-day,—" of worry," says the unromantic English reader.

It was, likewise, at Blidah, famous for its orange groves, under the spurs of the Atlas, that I came across 'Buth, par Madame Gaskell, auteur de Marie Barton, etc./ while the military band was drumming and fifing with might and with main all sorts of wild and warlike melodies, uncongenial enough to the clacking mills of Manchester, or the purple hills of peaceful Wales. Nowhere does the penetrative power of literature appear in more impressive contrast than in the French colonies of Northern Africa. As I looked round the place, where Jews, Arabs, and *militaires* were sitting in pairs upon the benches, I felt a great temptation to buy 'Ruth' there and then, and present it, with its African perfume of orange-blossoms, to Madame Gaskell, and was only deterred by the idea of dragging the volume over sea

and land for some fifteen hundred miles, ere it could reach its English destination.

Another great contrast of these African towns is seen in the shops for the clothing of the different sections of the population. In one magazine are bernouses, leather shoes of bright red and yellow, rope girdles, coarse cloth jackets, inlaid with gaudy stars, and Jewish coifs and stomachers, rich with gold thread. Round the corner is a little French *modiste's;* Paris collars and ribbons, light kid-gloves, lace, coloured silk handkerchiefs, and a handsome French baby, sitting up as good as gold, in splendid bibs and tuckers, it wide open eyes taking accurate note of the phenomena of French colonization in Algeria.

But I am wandering a long way from Carthage, from which I am yet only a "day's journey." But it is a very different day from that of the patriarch; being the evening and the morning of a very good French steamer. We left Bona at noon, passing on our way to the boat many parties of Arab women, stalking about in a ghastly blue costume, swathed up from head to feet, only *one* eye peeping out to enable them to pick their way over the rough aUeys.

Leaving the harbour, we sailed past the site of ancient Hippo, where lived and died one of the greatest Fathers of the early Christian Church,—St. Augustine. Some huge ruins, apparently those of water-cisterns, yet remain, and a tomb which bears the name of the saint, but his body is believed to be at Pavia, in Italy. It is recorded that, on the siege of Hippo by the Vandals under Genseric, St. Augustine prayed to God that he might be taken away before the city fell into the hands of the enemy; whereupon he was cut off during the siege by a violent fever. This was in the year 430.

We left Bona at noon, March 16th. The day was calm and lovely; and never shall I forget how twilight fell that evening. The heavens were divided as into two opposite camps of light and darkness, sunset and night, with a sharpness of division at the zenith wholly unknown to our northern latitudes; and

when Venus rose, she cast a long track of light upon the sea. It was nearly the date of the brightest night of the brightest year, and I sat on the deck till the heavy dews fell drenching around me, and the western glow had faded into the blue gloom. When at length I went below, I found all the officers and ship's passengers assembled round Herr Max Bcihrer, the famous German violinist, who was unpacking his beloved instrument, much as a mother would lift her child from the cradle; and there he sat and played "Home, sweet home," "Yankee doodle," " Partant pour la Syne," and " God save the Queen," till full night fell upon the shores of Africa, and shrouded the wild hills from even the man at the helm. When I awoke, we were at anchor in the Bay of Carthage.

On reaching the deck, a fine but most desolate scene presented itself. At the distance of half a mile lay Goletta, the port of Tunis, a small strip of buildings, arsenal, custom-house, fort, two "palaces," and a few smaller dwelling-houses. To the left, at the further end of a long, shallow, salt-water lake or lagune, lay Tunis, shining white in the morning sun, and about ten miles distant; to the right the grassy, uneven plain, backed by low hills, where once stood Carthage; a bluff headland, near which is the modern village of Carthagcna, lay beyond, still further to the right. The panorama was nearly encircled by mountains; the chain was carried out by precipitous islands rising from the sea. The odd shape of these mountains is hardly to be described, except by saying, that they reminded me of cheese that has been cut by a knife. I never saw so many straight lines and approximate right angles in a hill-chain before.

After long delay by the slow-boated Turks, we were at length landed at Goletta, and received by M. Cubisol, who acted as both French and English Consul. As we passed along the quay, we observed the pure Mussulman and half-savage look of the buildings and peojle, compared even to Algiers,—queer painted houses; wood-work of scarlet, yellow, and all smart hues; and little, dwarfish, Tunisian soldiers keeping guard, and looking at the European strangers with an air half-lazy, half-ferocious.

We were much nearer the site of ancient Carthage than we were to the city of Tunis, and, therefore, determined to visit the latter while yet the heat of the day had scarcely commenced. On March 16th the temperature of northern Africa was about equal to that of our warm summer days.

M. Cubisol, our consul, promised to see to our luggage, and we were soon seated in a hired carriage and *en route* for Carthage. Such a carriage! It was a degree worse than the worst of Algerine omnibuses. This was a vehicle with four seats, and a roof which could be put up or down at pleasure, and the driver's seat was also protected from the sun, the whole an unutterably shabby turn-out. I saw afterwards various other forms of carriage at Tunis, evidently of European build, and reduced to the last stage o f vehicular existence; giving the idea that the Bey was in the habit of buying-up cheap, every old phaeton, barouche, *caliche,* or cab, that had been pronounced unfit for use by Parisian authority.

We soon reached the edge of the grassy field where lie, bleaching in the sun of centuries, the scattered bones of murdered Carthage. It can hardly be called a plain, as there is, on the whole, a gentle inclination towards the sea. We made first for the house cf Mr. Davis, who was excavating for the British Museum, and who resided with his wife and children in a square erection of quite modern build. The nearest habitations to his were a bath and mosque, close together and of dazzling whiteness. I call them habitations because there are always residents attached to these Mohammedan institutions. From this point we took a general view of the ground, which swells up and down, broken here and there by rugged lumps of ruin. Nothing approaching to an entire ancient edifice is to be seen, and the massive fragments which rise above the turf are to be attributed to the later times of Roman occupation. Every vestige of

Punic Carthage lies under the level of the present soil, overgrown with grass, asphodel, and tare.

The immediate foreground was occupied by Mr. Davis's garden, a gentle horticultural pretence with which the English ladies were unwilling to dispense. Close to his house he had caused pits to be sunk,—pits from fifteen to twenty feet deep,—which appeared to lead to certain ancient tombs; for bones and pottery were brought up, and lay about the displaced earth. Some of the gentlemen went down by a rope; but the aperture was narrow, and the descent difficult for a woman, so I did not go down. In the house was a miscellaneous collection of articles,—beads, little idols, and fragments of glass, which latter peel, from decomposition, into thin lamine, and exhibit beautiful prismatic colours. There was also a small black stone, inscribed with Punic letters as yet undeciphered. The Bey stipulates that any articles composed of the precious metals shall be paid for if found, otherwise he appears to leave the investigation unmolested. On the ground-floor of Mr.

Davis's house were certain mosaics on a large scale, intended for the British Museum. One design represented a priestess,—Dido, perhaps. I apprehend that considerable doubt must exist as to whether they belong to Punic or to Roman days. Many of these mosaics had been carefully backed by new cement, otherwise they would have crumbled in their removal to England.

Leaving the house we proceeded towards the famous cisterns, which, with the exception of an aqueduct, form the only remains of Punic Carthage in tolerable preservation. The road, as I said before, is very unsafe; and though we had one horse with us belonging to Mr. Davis, he was soon led by the bridle, riderless. Here and there is a cultivated field, but the greater part of the ground, so far as I could observe, is rough with the remains of antiquity, and treacherous with deep holes, through which the pedestrian might at any moment fall headlong some twenty feet into a black oblivion. Either these cavernous

abysses were the cellars and cisterns of the ancient houses (such were sure to be an important feature in the architecture of that burning chmate), or else the lower storeys yet standing have been gradually buried in the course of ages by accumulated rubbish. This has happened in Rome to an astonishing extent; and the foundations of ancient London lie far beneath the present level of Chepe. The field of Carthage being thickly overgrown with a low but luxuriant vegetation; tall grasses, brambles, and many bright and beautiful flowers,—the reader may imagine that it proves rather dangerous walking.

Presently the traveller is called upon to descend a sloping excavation towards certain vaulted holes or chambers, and finds himself at the extremity of the enormous range of cisterns, seventeen in number, side by side, with vaulted roofs, and made accessible by two corridors running along either end. These are yet partially filled with water, and are lighted by shafts from above. The masonry is of Cyclopean size, and the grand masses of light and shadow surpass any effects I have seen in architecture. There appears now no doubt that these remains are those of public cisterns; though Lady Mary Wortley Montague says that they were thought in her time to be elephants' stables. I subjoin an extract from her letter to the Abbe, written from Tunis 150 years ago, viz. July 31st, 1718.

"At Tunis we were met by the English consul, who resides there. I readily accepted the offer of his house for some days, being very curious to see this part of the world, and particularly the ruins of Carthage. I set out in his chaise at nine at night, the moon being at full. I saw the prospect of the country almost as well as I could have done by daylight, and the heat of the sun is now so intolerable that it is impossible to travel at any other time. The soil is for the most part sandy, but everywhere fruitful of date, olive, and fig-trees, which grow without art, yet afford the most delicious fruit in the world. About six miles from Tunis we saw the remains of that noble aqueduct which carried the water to.

Carthage over several high mountains, the length of forty miles. There are still many arches entire. We spent two hours viewing it with great attention; and Mr. Wortley assured me that of Rome is very much inferior to it. The stones are of a prodigious size, and yet all polished, and so exactly fitted to each other, that very little cement has been made use of to join them. Yet they may probably stand a thousand years longer, if art is not made use of to pull them down. Soon after daybreak I arrived at Tunis...

.

"I went very early yesterday morning (after one night's repose) to see the ruins of Carthage. I was, however, half-broiled in the sun, and overjoyed to be led into one of the subterranean apartments, which they called, 'the stables of the elephants/ but which I cannot believe were ever designed for that use. I found in them many broken pieces of columns of fine marble, and some of porphyry. I cannot think anybody would take the insignificant pains of carrying them thither, and I cannot imagine such fine pillars were designed for the use of stables. I am apt to believe they were summer apartments under their palaces, which the heat of the climate rendered necessary. They are now used as granaries by the country people.

"When I was a little refreshed by rest, and some milk and exquisite fruit they brought me, I went up the little hill where once stood the castle of Byrsa, and from thence I had a distinct view of the situation of the famous city of Carthage, which stood on an isthmus, the sea coming on each side of it."

Although the learned abbe who was correspondent to the lively Lady Mar-, may have known all about the history of Carthage too well to have needed any further particulars from her pen, there may be some among our readers to whom a few historical notes in connection with our present subject may not be unacceptable. We have to go back nearly a thousand years before Christ, to the time when Dido, " granddaughter to the famous (or infamous) Jezebel," came from Phoenician Tyre, and purchased from the native inhabitants "only

so much land as an ox's hide would compass," which hide she acutely cut into strips. Here she built a citadel called Byrsa. It is quite immaterial that this tale is "exploded by the learned." For the rest, Dido's unhappy love-affair with neas, and her suicide upon the funeral pyre, are very old stories. Many of our readers will remember the anecdote of Porson, who, when some one defied him to make poetry out of the Latin gerunds, replied quick as thought,—

"When Dido found.tineas would not come,
She wept in silence, and was *Di, do, dum.*"

To come to a more authentic class of facts. The English traveller who sails into that lovely bay, girded by its quaint mountains, where now reigns a deep and desolate silence, will not forget that here rose and flourished and decayed the *greatest maritime nation of antiquity*. It is enough to make him accept Macaulay's famous prophecy of the New Zealander gazing at St. Paul's from the ruins of London Bridge, when he remembers that here was once all the bustling life of a thronged seaport, "lined with large quays, in which were distinct receptacles for securing and sheltering from the weather 220 vessels. The city had high walls and splendid temples, and all kinds of accommodation for the seamen." It had its Bermondsey and Blackwall, its huge St. Katharine's Docks, and doubtless, too, its Greenwich Hospital; magazines and storehouses containing all necessaries for the arming and equipping of fleets; and near the old port was a temple of A. pollo, with a statue of the god in massive gold. At the beginning of the Punic War the city had 700,000 inhabitants. Livy says it was twenty-three miles round; and as I looked over the plains from an eminence, I seemed to see no end of the ruin.

"Aristotle speaks of dinners given by various societies, probably like our clubs, in which political questions were discussed." And, lo! politics and clubs and club-goers are mingled alike with the grass of the field; and only Mr. Davis, digging away at the stricken

roots of Carthage, might hear, if he listens rightly, the sobbing sigh of past greatness, like that of fabled Mandragore.

Mr. W. Torrens M'Cullagh, in his 'Industrial History of Free Nations,' says, "The earliest commercial treaty, whereof any memorial has been preserved, was one between the Carthaginians and Etruscans. When as yet Mount Aventine was a wolf-walk, and in the clefts of the Tarpeian rock eagles of but inarticulate and undisciplined rapacity had as yet brought forth their young,—the Etruscans were the most influential race in Italy. They are linked to the Carthaginians by the bonds of reciprocal traffic; the exports and imports between them are carefully regulated by treaties; courts of justice are jointly established, where the citizens of one state may sue for redress of injuries inflicted by those of another." *(Vide* Aristotle.)

Among the Greeks, too, "Many Greeks traded to Carthage, and the Punic merchant is spoken of in comedy as one of a class familiarly known at Athens."

But there is a special interest attaching to this deserted plain in English eyes. From hence sailed the bold traders who bought our Cornwall tin, and then tried hard to keep the mines a secret from all the rest of the mercantile world. So amiable were the Phoenician cousins of Carthage, that while they knew more about the Mediterranean than any other people, and had explored far beyond the Gates of Hercules, usually held to be "the terminus of human adventure and aspiration," Mr. Grote informs us that "their jealous commercial spirit induced them to conceal their track, to give information designedly false respecting dangers and difficulties, *and even to drown any commercial rivals when they could do so with safety* (?). Strabo relates that a Phoenician captain, returning from Britain, was pursued by a Roman galley, and ran his own vessel on the rocks that the Roman might be tempted into the same destruction, and he did this that the enemy might not discover where he had been; and what was his cargo—British tin! This metal is supposed to have been also found in the Scilly Isles, then called *Cassiterides.* Heeren says, that the ore dug up on the mainland "was carried to the small islands lying off the Land's End, accessible to wagons at the time of ebb-tide."

What all this tin was wanted for is not so clear; but "the Phoenicians were celebrated for their skill in the art of dyeing; and the Tyrian purple, which was either a bright crimson or a scarlet, was held in the highest estimation. Hence it has been conjectured, with much probability, that the Phoenicians were acquainted with the use of the solution of tin in the preparation of that colour." Their mirrors were also made of copper and tin mingled together.

In Mr. Grote's History of Greece are many picturesque and interesting allusions to Carthage and her parent. He says, vol. iii. p. 366, "The Greek word 'Phoenicians' being used to signify as well the inhabitants of Carthage as those u of Tyre and Sidon, it is not easy to distinguish what belongs to each of them-but from the coast of Palestine to the coast of Cornwall there was no merchant-ship to buy or sell goods except those Phoenicians. The relations between mother and child were ever amicable, so far as they have come to our knowledge. At her period of highest glory Carthage sent messengers with a sacred tribute to Hercules of Tyre, during the siege of the latter town by Alexander the Great; and the women and children were sent from the beleaguered city to the protecting care of the colony, who thus repaid a debt of two centuries' standing; for when Cambyses was bent on conquering Carthage, the Tyrians refused their fleet.

Sign of harbour there is none upon this desolate shore at the present day, and the contour of the coast is somewhat altered; but from the elevated site of a Tunisian fort close to the sea are still to be seen, ineflaceably stamped upon the hill-side, the broad lines of an ancient flight of steps. Overgrown with grass and flowers, they yet retain a grand architectural resemblance, and nothing which I saw at Carthage struck me with so profound a sense of forlorn contrast. These steps, what were they? Did they lead up to a temple of Apollo, with its god of massive gold; or down to the quay, thronged with the bustling feet of many nations? And how comes it that their ghostly outlines yet remain, when city and seaport are utterly vanished? Is it that in the warm, blue, starry midnights of the African shore, mysterious processions yet file upwards and downwards, and wandering over the grassy plain, and by the murmuring tideless Mediterranean, recall with mournful wonder those fateful words, Delenda Est Carthago?

Such as I have now described it, must have been, with but little difference, the scene which met the French crusaders when they landed before Tunis. It remains to tell how France came to erect that memorial chapel to commemorate an event since which eight long centuries have now elapsed.

It was on the third Friday of Lent, the 14th of March, 1270, that King Louis IX., having sent his equipage on before, went out to St. Denis, and took the banner of the oriflamme from the altar, and, after many prayers, returned again to Paris, where, on the following day, he went on foot from his palace to the Cathedral of Notre Dame. On the Sunday he parted from his wife, Marguerite de Provence, she who had accompanied her husband on the first long Crusade, but who now saw him depart with three of her sons for an expedition, whose dangers she could realize only too well. The royal party travelled south by Melun, Sens, Macon, Lyons, Vienne, Avignon,—whose white walls and towers reminded them of an Eastern town. At Aigues-Mortes they embarked on the royal ship 'Le Paradis.' A dreadful storm they met in the Gulf of Lyons, and they tossed about *en route* for Sardinia and the little port of Cagliari, which at last they reached, and remained eight days there, though St. Louis did not leave his vessel, but busied himself in reconsidering his will, and adding a codicil, which is dated, "In nave nostra juxta Sardiniam." In a great council held by him, it was here decid-ed to make way for Tunis, whose ruler, Mohammed, was not unfriendly. It was said that he had even manifested some desire to become a Christian; and it was hoped that he might allow the Crusaders to pass through his dominions on their way to the Holy Land. fco on the 21st of July, the naval force found itself in sight of Tunis, fifteen miles south-west from the ruins of Carthage, and as they entered the bay they saw distinctly the remains of aqueducts, and great compact blocks under the water, and also remains of a square plat form, with "heaps of jasper, porphyry, and serpentine." Here, said tradition, was the palace of Dido; and going towards Cape Carthago, they found upon the shore a large circular tower, and walls forming a long square. But of the statue of Cato of Utic-fi, his naked sword in hand, or of Marius, Scipio, Hannibal, Belisarius, no memento existed; neither palace nor image. "Their shades were mute upon the plains where once was Carthage the Great." Here and there were modern Moorish buildings, and a fortress, with an embattled tower; of this Louis hoped to gain possession; while vast plantations of figs and olives offered a desirable shelter for the troops. But Mohammed was less favourable than had been hoped for; and on the 19th of July, a prodigious number of Saracens poured from the interior on to the shore, but took to flight as the royal galley, heading a portion of the fleet, sailed into the bay. In a few hours the tents were disposed iu the midst of a vast plain, and all was arranged for an orderly camp, except that nobody thought of assuring themselves of the presence of fresh water. Some cisterns were found at a distance, but the young sailors who were sent there fell in with a party of Saracens, who, "emerging from neighbouring caverns, fell upon them and murdered them without mercy." So exactly this description tallies with the present state of the plain.

Now began much fighting, the Moors keeping in the caves, where many of them were smoked to death by the French soldiers, just as the company of Arabs were by Pelissier during the recent war in Algiers; and the army after this obtained some days of repose. But on the Friday night, when their Sabbath was over, the natives again appeared in great numbers, and close to the camp. And so it went on for many days, until the army, suffering from the climate and from continual harass, began to show signs of contagious disease. The want of fit food, and still more of fit water, made awful havoc in a short time; and the Arabs took to raising clouds of sand in the immediate vicinity of the camp, which caused frightful distress. In the midst of it all the king went from tent to tent among the dead and the dying, quite regardless of his personal safety. The first name inscribed on the black list is Matthieu de Montmorency; he " passed from life to death on the 1st of August." Then Henri de Beaujeu, Marshal of France; the Comte de Venddme, the Comte de la Marche, Hugries de Lusignan, Gauthier de Nemours, Raoul de Nesle. Great names all; and many more than I can copy. Then the sons of the king fell sick, and then the king! The young Prince Jean Tristan was taken ill on shipboard, where he died. He was only twenty-five, having been born at Damietta during the first Crusade. No longer seeing1 the young man at his bedside, St. Louis guessed wherefore, and forced his confessor to tell him the truth. "Such was his resignation, that to see it was to feel that the separation would be but for a few days." He ordered the body of bis son to be enclosed in a precious coffin, and taken to the Church of Royaumont in France.

Meanwhile the king became worse, while one after another of the great lords of France fell victims around him. Three doctors,—Jean Pitard, Pierre de la Brosse, and le chanoine Dudon,—did their best to save him, but he turned him to his chaplains, and begged them to pray by his side, giving to the elder his book of Psalms, "which would be of no more use to him."

Now came the ambassadors of Michael Paleologus, and he received them round his bed with a calm face, and when they were gone, called to him the eldest of his sons, Philippe de

France, who, having also been very ill, was now convalescent; and to him he gave long advice on the way in which he should rule his people; and to his daughter Agnes he wrote a letter, which he gave to Thibaut, his son, to deliver.

It was on the 25th of August,—henceforth to be famous in France as the Fete St. Louis,—that the folds of the royal tent, sprinkled with the fleur-de-lys, were seen to open, and the dying monarch issued thence, clothed in a long white robe, a cross between his livid hands, and his eyes fixed upon the bed of ashes spread upon the dry, bare ground. And thereon, at three in the afternoon, surrounded by what remained of his weeping court and family, he died; and thereon he lay, while his brother the King of Sicily's fleet came over the blue waters to join the French force, to whose first eager inquiry a man-at-arms replied, "Jamais vif ne le reverrey."

He was buried at St. Denis; but on the plain of Carthage is the memorial chapel which consecrates the spot of earth whereon he died.

THE TERRACE OF ST. GERMAIN. rjIHE stateliest walk which man hath made—
Imperial Rome no equal shows—
Is that which casts a league of shade
Where Seine amidst her meadows flows.
Spring clothes its cyclopean wall Of living forest every year,
And Autumn drapes a splendid pall
  For nature as the days grow drear.
  And though it was the hand of Art
  Which shaped and wrought the royal plan,
  Yet Nature brought her nobler part
To dignify the work of man.
  It sweeps athwart the level hill, As if for giant footsteps meant;
What King but here might gaze his fill,
  And pace the mighty path content!
  Yet here a kingly Exile came,
To brood on sorrows day by day;
  Of daughters who abjured his name,
And three fair kingdoms passed away.
  A dark and melancholy soul
His pictures show, as if he saw
  The writing of some fatal scroll,
The sentence of some ruthless law;

And knew his Father's blood had made
A vain libation for the race, Whose last lone Son should lay his head
Uncrowned within the sacred place
Where nations worship, and should owe Unto the king who wore his crown,
  Canova's tomb of moulded snow,
And words whereby his state is known.
  Sad English Ghost! whose line decayed
On English page scarce owns a friend!
  With what pathetic steps ye tread
The lordly walk from end to end!
THE FOUNTAIN OF GUINGAMP.
JJANDSOME young Louis XV. was fast changing into a middle-aged spectacle, contemned of gods and men, when in the year 1743 the good people of Guingamp, in Brittany, resolved to rebuild the fountain of their marketplace. This fountain was then nigh upon three hundred years old, having been originally constructed by Due Pierre, the husband of St. Francoise d'Amboise. Pierre was an unstable sort of character, and he treated his angelic wife much as the Marquis treated Griselda. It might indeed be supposed that he had read, in his boyhood, the first edition of Chaucer, and had resolved to enact, on his own account, that celebrated conjugal drama; for, like the Marcpais Walter, he seemed to think her sweet bearing was— "of 8om subtiltee
And of malice, or for cruel corage
That she had suffered this with sad visage;"
and he behaved so shamefully, in his fits of causeless jealousy, that angry Breton barons, who came from right and left to remonstrate with him, might well inquire—
"What coud a sturdy husbond more devise
To preve hire wifhood, and hire stedfastnesse,
And he continuing ever in sturdinesse P"

But there came a day when Due Pierre repented, and having brought his wife to the verge of the grave by his violence, grace touched his heart; and he fell on his knees by her bedside, with tears in his eyes and prayer on his lips. Then of course Francoise instantly forgave him, and embraced him, saying, "Monseigneur, mon amy, je vous le pardonne de bon coeur, ne pleurez plus, car je scais bien que cette malice n'est point venue de vous, mais de l'ennemy de nature, qui est envieux de nostre bien et de la felicite a laquelle nous tendons. " And thereafter Due Pierre was really a changed man (it is particularly specified that he got up at four o'clock every morning), and, like Chaucer's couple—

"Ful many a yere in high prosperitee Liven these two in concord and in rest;" and not only so, but he aided his pious duchess in her good works, and among other benefactions to the town of Guingamp, where they dwelt in a "little castle," he built this fountain, bringing the water in pipes from a neighbouring hill, through a street which was from thence called *la Rim de la Pompe.*

And this fountain, having been frequently mended up, and having cost the town (according to the public accounts) *quinze sous* in 1464, for soldering the pipes, *cinq sous* in 1465, in compensation for injury done by laying said pipes, again twenty crowns (by subscription of twenty rich burgesses) to further repairs of the conduit, and one hundred crowns in 1588 (which the mayor borrowed of the Abbot of St. Croix) for the reconstruction of the monument itself, and for repurchasing an angel of stone, which had somehow strayed into the possession of one widow Rene Rocancour, was now, in 1743, no longer mendable. And therefore the town council resolved to have a new *pompe,* to bring the water from the hill of Montbareil on a long aqueduct, and to pay good hard money for a new basin and ornaments. The sum which they made up their minds to produce from the official purse does not seem large to our modern ears—*quinze cent livres,* sixty pounds in modern reckoning; but in Brittany, one hundred and twentythree years ago, it could not have been shabby, for Guingamp was and is a substantial little town, with a history and a reputation to sustain. To this end they made a bargain, registered on the 28th

of December, with Corlay, the celebrated sculptor of CMteaulandron. Bred a car penter, Corlay, in handling the tools, had discovered that he was born an artist; and as he was a local genius, whose fame had, as it were, grown up under the very eyes of the burgesses of Guingamp (from which Chateaulandron was not above four leagues distant), it is much to their credit that they believed in the prophet of their own country. The result amply justified their choice. The reader is therefore requested to transport his spiritual vision to Chateaulandron, a small town on the river LefF; to a house built with fantastic gable ends, and ornamented at the angle of each wall with little wooden figures; and to a low-ceiled room, where a person having the marked physiognomy of the extreme north-west of France—a dark-eyed man clad in a complete suit of black velvet—sat before a portfolio of drawings under the light of an oil lamp. Those were days when gentlemen of degree wore immense periwigs, and the most famous sculptor of Brittany might reasonably have adopted fashionable costume; but Corlay wore his own long black hair parted down the middle, *aptes la mode de Bretagne;* he was unashamed of his peasant birth, and his handsome garments were cut after the old pattern; a short vest, and immensely full breeches gathered to the knee; while the wide flapping hat, which lay on the table beside him, was of the shape which may yet be seen in the market of Quimper or at the Pardon of Ploermel.

As Corlay turned over the loose leaves and innumerable scraps of paper which accumulate in an artist's portfolio, the most beautiful Gothic designs were lit up one after another. Most of them were sketches taken in the towns of his native province; here a tower in the pure simple ogival, there a chapel blossoming with the fantastic wealth of the renaissance. There were *calvairet,* each rich with a population of sacred personages; and bits of streets and markets fringed with gable ends, beneath which the deep doorways seemed purposely retreating into shadow to veil the romantic histories within. One lovely

drawing showed a strong stone turret embroidered with fine patterns, dating perhaps from *Francois premier,* or earlier, and now garlanded with a brilliant creeper rooted in the court below; and there were also many statues, as of blessed Charles de Blois, clad in armour as when he fell at Auray, and of the meek matron St. Francoise d'Amboise. But none of these drawings seemed to be exactly what Corlay wanted, and at last he rose, and taking up his large circular hat, he sallied forth into the moonshine.

In the early part of the last century, the towns of Brittany were untouched by the hand of the spoiler. No convenient but destructive road of iron had linked them with the throbbing heart of France. The gable-ended houses cut sharply against the starry sky; their angles broken by carved figures of saint and hero, and their sides covered with scaly slates, as though "mermen bold" had come from La Manche and Morbihan to advise in their construction. Here and there, where the upper storeys overhung very much, the narrow way was plunged in absolute darkness; but the little statues on the gables overhead stood out like silver in the moonshine. Corlay passed through CMteaulandron till he came quite outside the town on the western suburb, to a low stone house whose roof hardly overtopped the walled garden. The month was October, and he could see the apples glistening here and there on the trees, and hear the chill breezes whispering in a tall poplar behind the house. He knocked sharply at the garden door, which, after a cautious glance through a small barred aperture, was opened by a stout serving girl in full Breton costume; her high white cap shone like snow in the moonlight, as Corlay traversed the garden, where the late roses hung their heads in anticipation of frost, while the leaves crackling under his feet bore witness that

"The melancholy days were come, the saddest of the year,
Of naked woods and wailing winds, and meadows brown and sere,"
or rather that those days were approach-

ing rapidly; for there were still a few lingering flowers, and on the morrow would gleam a few warm sunbeams, strangely typical of the home life within that old house.

Corlay, who was a tall man, stooped as he passed under the low arch of the doorway which admitted him into a square panelled hall. It was perfectly plain; neither weapons of warfare nor spoils of the chase adorned its walls, nor, which was more remarkable, were there to be seen any of those portraits in pastille or in oil in which the French of the upper class so much delighted. The only ornaments were two palms crossed above the fireplace, artificially wrought with straw, such indeed as are to this day carried in St. Peter's on Palm Sunday. The room on the right, to which Corlay was ushered, was also plain even to bareness. It might easily be divined that this house had no master, and that the two frail female forms bending over their needles were far from rich in worldly goods. They were, nevertheless, not quite alone; by the side of the fire sat an aged priest, clad in the long full gown worn by the Jesuits in those days; he was indeed so old that his person was shrunk, and his face immobile save for the fiery dark eyes of Brittany which gleamed beneath his long white eyebrows.

The mistress of the house rose as Corlay entered, and the light upon the table, between her seat and the door, cast up its faint radiance upon a face it would not have been easy to forget, though it was neither young nor, strictly speaking, beautiful. Her age may have been about fifty, perhaps a little less. She was dressed in the quaint fashion of Breton widowhood; but the stuff was old and rusty as her features were thin and worn. The hair was white; the eyes, dark and naturally passionate, wore an expression of habitual resignation, over which would sometimes flash a look of fear, as if memory had evoked some terrible scene of which the images could never quite be laid to sleep. On her left hand was a worn wedding ring, absolutely her only ornament, if such it could be called. This lady inclined her

head to Yves Corlay with the grace of a woman bred in the ranks of the *haute noblesse;* though nought in her surroundings nor in her plebeian name of Madame Moine argued a claim to birth or breeding.

The younger lady, who had been sitting with her back to the door, turned round with an indescribable faint joyousness, and held out both slender hands with an exclamation of welcome. Then it could be seen that she was slightly deformed, and that her face bore that spiritual wistful expression so often seen in connection with this misfortune. Corlay lifted his hat from his broad brows, and came forward with a touch of timidity, which showed where lay the strong man's love.

"I salute you, Madame Moine. Mademoiselle, I have the honour to kiss your hands," said the sculptor, with a profound reverence.

"Louise-Marie," said the old priest, in the feeble voice of extreme age, "give me my cloak, my child; the wind blows in from the garden."

Louise-Marie turned quickly and affectionately towards the speaker, wrapped him round in his large cloak, arranged the cushion which supported his feeble head, and showed by the touch of dutiful care in her manner, that she had been bred up in great observance towards him. As she moved she coughed slightly. Yves Corlay's anxious eyes followed her every gesture, noted the pallor of her delicate skin, and the weary yet vivacious pose of the little head, with its rolls of black hair. The mother caught his glance, and said, "It is Louise-Marie's birthday; Pere Nicolas has been able to spend it with the child of his adoption. He has known her so long—so long!"

"Three-and-twenty years to-night, my little daughter," said the old man affectionately; "three-and-twenty years this 25th of October, since I baptized you in mortal haste, thinking you would surely die. But you lived! my little Louise-Marie, you lived! And you will say a few prayers now and then over the grave of your old friend for the good service he rendered you three-and-

twenty years ago."

Madame Moine shivered from head to foot, as she said, half aloud to herself, "And I was not yet four-and-twenty years old!"

Corlay looked up with surprise and sympathy mingled in his eyes. He did not understand whence the pang arose; but Louise-Marie, leaning towards him, said in an almost inaudible whisper, "My poor father, he was dead; yes, he was already dead!"

Corlay was silent; he had never heard this before, and his heart thrilled with sympathy for the mother of the woman he loved. He now comprehended something of the sad domestic drama which bound these three people together; supposing that Pere Nicolas had been the spiritual friend of the family before the death of Monsieur Moine. But his acquaintance dated only two years back, at which period the two ladies had first appeared at Chateaulandron, and he had asked no questions as to their past. He only knew they had long been resident in Italy, and had lately returned to dwell in their native province.

"And with what is our celebrated Maitre Yves now busy?" asked Louise-Marie in her soft voice. (Yves Corlay was some twenty years older than herself, and she clung to his society with the enthusiasm of an Italian exile, as she almost might be considered, for her first memories were of Perugia and its glorious company of purple mountains.)

"Precisely, Mademoiselle, I have come to ask your amiable advice," said Corlay, in the simple French which was after all with him an acquired language, for he had been born and bred a Breton artisan. He went on, "The mayor and burgesses of Guingamp have resolved to rebuild the fountain in their market-place, originally placed there by Due Pierre, the husband of the blessed Francoise d'"Amboise. The pipes were so old that the community found repairs too costly, and once for all they have fetched water from the hill of Montbareil; and they have brought it on *arches,* Mademoiselle, arches which some do say recall to mind the Appian aqueduct "

Louise-Marie clapped her little hands with mild sarcasm. "As if anything *we* can build could in the least resemble those glorious remnants of ancient Rome." And she shut her eyes and recalled the long sweeps of the Campagna, barred with alternate light and shadows, and the jagged sunny outline of the Sabine hills, crowned by the higher Apennine beyond. Her long lashes were dimmed with tears as she said sweetly, "And how is the fountain to be built. Maitre Yves? and in what sort of market-place is it to be?"

"The market, Mademoiselle, is of a triangular shape, bordered by ancient houses, just like our own. Close by the fountain is a beautiful mountain ash-tree, with scarlet berries at this season of the year, which look charming against the blue sky, I can assure you; and just beyond to the east is a mansion with a pointed turret, and beyond that again are the towers and spire of the great church of Notre Dame, all built of solid granite."

"How pretty, Maitre Yves! as pretty, at least, as anything can be in this bleak north."

"Nay, child, do not speak so of the country of your birth," put in Pere Nicolas, with a flash in his old eyes which showed that eighty-five years had not dimmed the fervour of the patriot priest.

"What has Brittany given to *me*, father *V* said the gentle Louise-Marie, with a touch of irony in her voice. "You and my mother tell me I was born here, but I remember nothing in my infancy but the churches and gardens of my dearest Italy. I remember the ramparts of Perugia, and the angels of Perugino, and the vast miles of the olive and the vine; and of Brittany I know nought but sorrow, mystery, and "—she shuddered—" *perhaps disgrace." "*Her voice was broken with sharp coughing, and Father Nicolas said eagerly, "Nay, not disgrace, my child, not *that;"* while her mother, with a trembling accent, broke in with renewed questions about the great commission with which Corlay had been entrusted.

"I think to make it of a Gothic model," said he, "after the fashion of the cross which Jean de la Bataille long ago put up for the sorrowing English Edward at his town of Northampton. It shall have a slender canopy, and under it a spout from which the clear water shall come brimming down. But I can claim no kindred to-night with Alexander le Imagineur, whose work at Waltham they say mine doth much resemble, for to-night I can frame no details in my mind's eye." And his eye dwelt on Mademoiselle Moine with anxious foreboding.

"Nay," said she, "I can suggest fairer models than any which your French chisellers have wrought in that cold Normandy across the sea. In my own land there is no market-place without its clear jets of water; ncj. great sunny piazza unadorned by broad basins, round whose margins disport sea monsters or river gods. It is the country of the nymph and the naiad. They came thither when Greece became a conquered land, and made the inspiration of a race of artists four hundred years ago. Ah, Perugia, Sienna, Toscanella, Florence, Rome! I see your white walls festooned by the scarlet vine-leaves and your campaniles halftransparent to the blue sky, and under your unclouded heavens the beautiful uncovered fountains throwing up a million drops of diamonds and pearls."

She stopped, exhausted with her own warmth, and then said, smiling and half ashamed, "Bring me our engravings, Maitre Corlay." And he went obediently to a great oak chest which stood in a corner of the room, fetched out from thence a thick square volume, bound in faded red morocco, with a gilded coronet, and the letters P D emblazoned on one side.

Corlay carried this to the table and placed it under the circle of light, and opened it with a certain tender care. On the blank page was written in a fine upright Italian hand,—" Pietro Doria a son amie. Genes, 1739 -" and on the fine printed title-page it was set forth in Italian that the book contained engravings of the monuments in the different towns of Italy. They were indeed duplicates of that series by "some of the accomplished predecessors of Piranesi, who were skilled in perspective and architecture, and whose touches were firm and excellent," with which Goethe's father ornamented his anteroom about ten years later; and Corlay turned them over with fingers which lingered affectionately on every page. There was the mausoleum of Hadrian, whose foundations, laid in sunless depths below the Tiber, support such a mighty masonry; there was the bronze horse to which Michael Angelo said " Go on;" there was the obelisk on the Pincian Hill, which had lately been dug up from the Gardens of Sallust; and one which had already stood for one hundred and fifty years before the Lateran Basilica, but which was hewn long ere Israel left Egypt. And there were stiff-lined porticoes, done in that black bold style of the early engravers, and the great semicircular sweep of the Piazza of St. Peter's. On this engraving Corlay lingered long; for beside the great obelisk from the temple of the sun at Heliopolis, which had been finally placed in the piazza by the labour of eight hundred men and a hundred and fifty horses, there were the two flashing fountains, one on either hand.

Mademoiselle, however, put out her slender fingers, and turned over the leaves impatiently, till she came to the one she sought. It represented a vast Duomo in an Italian town—a church built of fine brick with ribbed string-courses, but coated on either side of the north door by marble wrought in a delicate diaper pattern. Over against the door was a small but elaborate pulpit, *outside,* so that the preacher could thence address those "standing in the market-place." From the door, one coming out would descend from a platform thirteen steps into the piazza, and find himself face to face with the fountain which occupied the foreground of the picture. This was composed of two basins, the upper and lesser supported on tiny pillars. Each basin was many-sided, with small panels; the lower panels had each a sacred bas-relief; the upper ones were divided by single figures of personages in Holy Writ. The whole was elevated upon four steps set upon a circular platform, and the water sprang from a centre ornament, and fell back into the upper basin. When the wind blew it would sprinkle the hot pavement of the piazza far and wide. Underneath was printed, "Fontana di Perugia."

Louise-Marie fixed eager eyes on the sculptor. "This," said she, "is the first thing that I can remember. Let it be an Italian fountain, Maitre Yves."

And she seized the chalk which the sculptor mechanically twisted in his hand, and began tracing rough lines upon paper. A slight sketch it was, slight and irregular, but suggesting the fine rounded proportions of Italian art; two large vases below, and surmounted by a figure, around which she struck half-curves like jets of water rising and falling.

"But," said her mother, " what will the good people of a town in Brittany think of an Italian fountain in the midst of the Gothic market-place V 'They will think it beautiful, Mamma, when Maitre Yves has worked out the design; and he will put the figure of the Blessed Virgin at the top instead of the broken angel of stone which he says was placed above the old one; and when I go into Guingamp I shall think I see a fountain in my dear Italy."

Maitre Yves Corlay proved obedient; he took home Louise-Marie's little sketch, and he worked out the most beautiful details. The design which he sent in to the burgesses comprised three basins: the lowest was of granite, encircled by a railing of wrought iron; the second was upborne by four sea-horses; the third by four sirens, and ornamented by heads of angels and dolphins; on the summit stood the Mother of Jesus, her feet resting on the crescent; twenty jets of water were represented as enveloping her like a veil. In the faces of the sirens and angels might be caught something of the Breton type; but the whole was "a thing of beauty," which carried the thoughts irresistibly to scenes of southern life. It was as Louise-Marie had desired.

The bargain for the execution of this fountain was registered on the 28th of December, 1743; you may see it in the archives of Guingamp whenever you happen to pass that way; and in the guide to the town you may read this sentence, "Corlay nous a donne tout simplement un petit chef-d'oeuvre de grace, de fantaisie, et d'originalite; rien ne porte la le cachet du dix-huitieme siecle; on dirait le caprice d'un Florentin du temps des Meclicis." And now you know how this came to be.

It was two years before the fountain was finished and set up where it now stands; but Louise-Marie lived to see its completion. Its waters played for the first time in July, 1745, on the night of the great annual *Pardon*, or religious fete of Guingamp. Her mother had brought her into Guingamp, and placed her on a couch at the window of one of the ancient houses overlooking the market. It was a lovely night, as it always is on the night of the *Pardon.* If it rains in the morning, say the peasants, it is sure to be fine in the evening of that first Saturday in July. Yves Corlay walked in the great procession which issued from the portal of Notre Dame as the clock struck nine. Like hundreds of fellow-pilgrims he carried a long torch, and chanted Breton hymns as he walked. He it was who fired the great bonfire in the market, which brought out his new fountain into such wonderful relief, and made the springing water look like fairy jewels. But his heart was sore and heavy even upon this night of triumph; and his hps seemed hardly able to form a prayer, for he had now no hope that Heaven would bestow the one gift— Louise-Marie's life. Through the months of early autumn Corlay watched her die; and at the last there came to the sick-bed of the Breton maiden two tall young men of Breton blood, of whom he had never heard before—her brothers; and an Italian stranger, sent for by Madame Moine; and he too waited patiently and tenderly; but Louise-Marie was chastened by long suffering now, and she grieved the kind sculptor by no open preference of the lover from whom she had been separated so long ago.

When all was over, when the three strangers had disappeared as mysteriously as they had come, and the lonely mother had retired to the Carmelites of Guingamp, Corlay was summoned to another deathbed—that of the venerable Pere Nicolas. The old priest was close upon ninety years of age, but his faculties were undimmed; and he told to Corlay the following tale, though at much greater length, adding that it was by Madame Moine's desire:—

In the year 1719 Brittany had been convulsed by a popular rising in defence of rights confiscated by the kings of France, who had only acquired that ancient province as a marriage dower, and who were never looked upon exactly as standing in the place of the old dukes. Numerous noble gentlemen were involved; it suffices to name MM. de Guer de Poncallec, de la Boessiere, Lambilly, du Couedic, de Melac-Henrieux, de Montlouci, the three brothers Talhouet, and the two Polducs, cadets of the Kohans. Of these, four were brought before the Chambre de Nantes on the Tuesday of Holy Week, 1720; and one of the four, M. le Moyne de Talhouet, had voluntarily given himself up, at the instance of his wife, who had been told that this step would ensure his safety. They were a young couple, with four little children, and another immediately expected.

Alas! the poor lady was cruelly deceived. The four gentlemen were tried, condemned, and executed in one single day; and the scene at the scaffold at the *Bouffay* was an awful one indeed. Each prisoner was attended by a separate confessor; Pere Nicolas walked beside Le Moyne Talhouet.

It was five in the morning when these gentlemen were brought out to die by torchlight.

The whole story is too long and too sad to be recounted here; but Pere Nicolas wrote it all out, and his writing has been published. After telling it to Corlay, however, he asked him to open a secretaire by his bedside, and bring out an old yellow letter, which he unfolded. It was from Madame le Moyne de Talhouet, written in reply to one of his own, telling her of the awful end. A more affecting letter was never penned:—

"Then my dear husband is dead, Reverend Father! and it has not been given me to receive his last sigh. O Father, how hard and bitter is the cup to my lips! How my heart bleeds! I have lost the best husband that ever was, and that by my fault. I was deceived, deceived, dear Father, and by officers who were themselves equally deceived, and I was unhappy enough to have persuaded him to go and give himself up into their hands, upon the assurance they had given me that this was the certain way to obtain his pardon. He obeyed blindly every wish of mine, and to my most insupportable woe, it was by our mutual love that he was thus lost. What did he say about this to you, 0 my dear Father? What did he say about the four poor orphans whom he has left to my care, with provision that does not amount to two hundred—no, not to one hundred—francs a year? Tell me, I beseech you, by the Holy Passion of our Saviour, all his feelings, and all that he said to you about me. How much I fear that he may have uttered some reproach on the unhappy counsel which I gave him! I beg of you, dear Father, since you were as father to my dear husband, tell me all he said to you of me and of our dearest children; tell me also if you feel sure that his good and generous soul has found grace with God. My love and my heart are with him, my Father, and if he is with God, I, too, would long to be already there also.

"What a sight am I, dear Father! a woman, not yet four-and-twenty years old! and to have lost a dear husband loved with a passion nigh to idolatry, to see him perish innocent of the crime of which he is accused, and perish by such a cruel and barbarous hand; and leave me with four poor little children, the eldest only five years old! See my sad estate! Happy, alas! had I been if he had never known me! Once more, dear Father, what did he say, and can you assure me that he is with the Lord? Why was I not happy enough to die at the same time and in the same manner? Say Masses for him; use for this purpose the money he gave you; I think that his soul will thus be comforted. Can you not by your prayers persuade the Lord to let me see and hear my dear Talhouet? 0 my Father, if there is compassion in your heart, get me this grace, and remember in all your prayers the most unhappy and desolate woman who was ever born. I will listen to any consolation you will give me; I love you because you received the last sigh of my dear husband.

"de Talhouet Le Moyne. "I forgot to tell you that my strongest desire is to die. Ask God to make me ready as my husband was, and take me from the world; my children will be looked to by their relations. Tell me what he said of me, and answer me quickly."

After the birth of her child, which proved to be a girl, the poor young widow left France, as she thought for ever. Pcre Nicolas sent her to the care of his sister, who was Superior of a convent at Perugia. She lived close to this convent, and brought up her daughter with the greatest difficulty; the child suffered from the grievous anguish her mother had endured previous to her birth. Two sons entered the Papal Guard; one died, and the fourth became a priest. She lived in profound retirement, dropping her aristocratic name, and in fear lest aught should recall her to the vindictive Regent of France, and bring down fresh misfortune on her head. When at last she came back to Brittany, it was partly on account of an estate of which the forfeiture was menaced through her absence, and partly to separate Louise-Marie from a young Genoese nobleman who assiduously sought her society, but whom the mother believed would never consent to wed her when he knew that her father had died a disgraced man upon the public scaffold. Perhaps in this matter Madame de Talhouet's fears were hardly just to Pietro Doria.

The reader knows the rest. Pere Nicolas died, and a few years after, Madame de Talhouet, who was not yet sixty, was laid to rest in the cemetery of the convent. Corlay did not marry; but he lived to be quite an old man. In the year when the lovely Dauphiness of fifteen entered France, which to her was to prove so fatal, the sculptor received a visit from a dear Italian friend. Corlay's long curling hair lay white about his shoulders; the Italian was younger by only half a generation; but his eye had not forgotten the fire of his youth. Together the two men stood by the fountain of Guingamp, whose waters had been rising and falling for a quarter of a century. It was as if a symbol of her beloved Italy had sprung up at Louise-Marie's behest under the gables of the old Gothic market-place, and beneath the shadow of the granite towers of Notre Dame; and each stood bareheaded in the sunshine, as though the place were holy, and said a prayer for the woman whom both had loved so well.

PBINTED BY J. E. TATLOB AND CO., LITTLE QUEEN STBEET, LINCOLN'S INN FIELDS.

Lightning Source UK Ltd.
Milton Keynes UK
UKOW06f1807270115

245214UK00012B/811/P